Patterns of REVISION

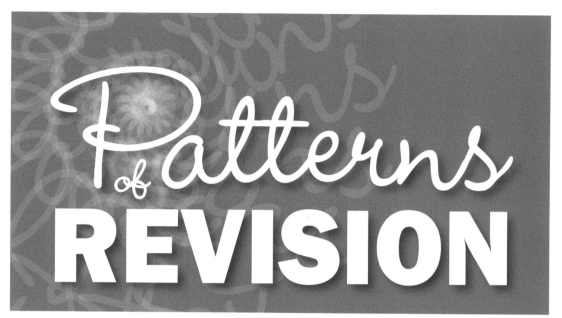

Patterns of REVISION

Inviting 3rd GRADERS into Conversations That Elevate Writing

Whitney La Rocca & Jeff Anderson

Routledge
Taylor & Francis Group

NEW YORK AND LONDON

A Stenhouse Book

Cover design and interior design by Page2, LLC, Wayne, NJ

First published 2024
by Routledge
605 Third Avenue, New York, NY 10158

and by Routledge
4 Park Square, Milton Park, Abingdon, Oxon, OX14 4RN

Routledge is an imprint of the Taylor & Francis Group, an informa business

ISBN: 9781625316318 (pbk)
ISBN: 9781032681986 (ebk)

DOI: 10.4324/9781032681986

Typeset in ITC Berkeley Oldstyle, ITC Franklin Gothic Std, Wendy LP Std
by Page2, LLC, Wayne, NJ

Access the Support Material: www.routledge.com/9781625316318

For my writing partners who help to make revision magical.

– Whitney

For people living with Parkinson's and those who help them thrive.

– Jeff

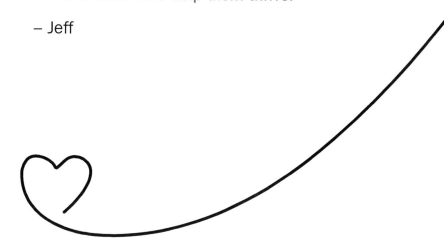

Contents

Part 2 **Revision Through Sentence Combining**   **125**

Putting DRAFT Together   **127**

Acknowledgments

We are incredibly grateful to everyone who helped bring *Patterns of Revision* to life. Without the help of teachers willing to join us in trying out some of our ideas, we would never have been able to create truly practical lessons for the classroom. With the feedback we received, we revised, revised, and revised some more. This book is a direct result of the magic of revision.

Huge thanks to Kathleen Joerger Lindsey Elementary School and Manford Williams Elementary School in Lamar Consolidated Independent School District including Sherri Hatton, Jackie Castillo, Barbara Andrzejewksi, Anisa Garza, Heather Williams, Sarah Ramirez, and Christie Burch. Your children were such a delight, and your feedback helped to really shape these lessons early on. Your support for this work continues to be truly appreciated. Thank you to Cassye Baker, Euberta Lucas, Kallie Roman, and Kiana Johnson at McElwain Elementary and to Julia Arcuri, Lori Davies, and Jessie Miller at Davidson Elementary in Katy Independent School District for opening your doors to help us fine-tune the *Patterns of Revision* lesson structure. To Jennifer Hamrick, Debbie Poole, and Dana Boozer at Pelion Elementary School in Lexington County School District One, thank you for piloting some of our lessons. You have some stars in this book!

We also had so many teachers and friends submit writing samples for us to use during our research, deciding which lessons could be most effective for third graders.

Stenhouse continues to be such a support system for us. Thank you so much to Emily Hawkins, Stefani Roth, Stephanie Levy, Shannon St. Peter, and Lynne Costa for your continued love and care you give to our *Patterns* family. Mark Overmeyer, thank you for being an additional eye on this project. Thank you to our entire editing and design team for turning our plain manuscript into this beautiful book.

Travis Leech, you were a crucial piece to this puzzle! Thank you for the many brainstorming sessions, the template and chart creations, the mockups, and the many revisions of each of them. We are so glad to have you on our team.

To our brilliant editor, Terry Thompson, how do we even say thank you? It needs to be so much more. You have been beyond patient and flexible through this process, always giving us time to work through lesson template after template, design note after design note, and leading us in the right direction, always providing feedback and questions that truly helped shape this work. We absolutely could not have done this without you. We love you.

To our families, thank you for putting up with us, especially when we had deadlines hanging over us! You continue to be our biggest cheerleaders, and we are so thankful to have you in our lives. Love you so much!

– Whitney and Jeff

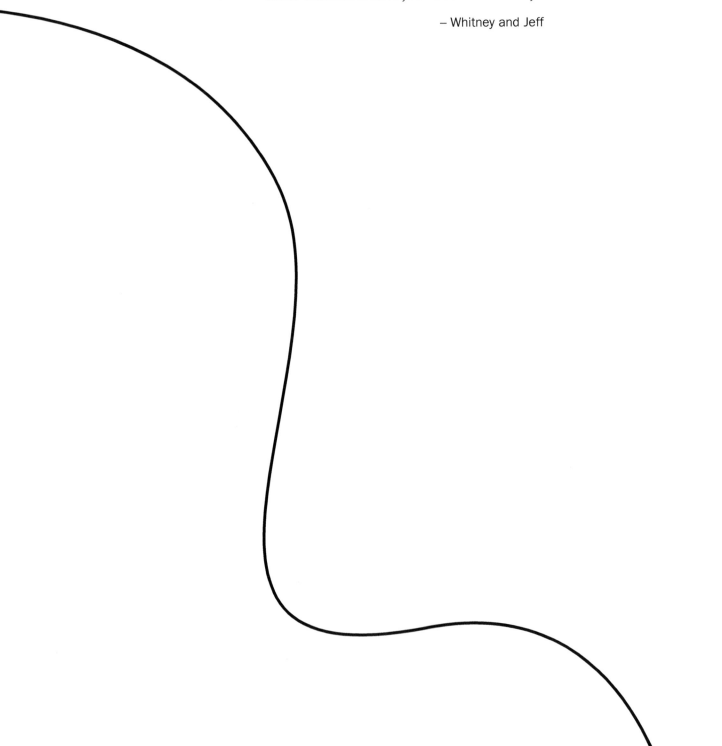

Introduction

OWNING the *Patterns of Revision*

Remember one thing: That you should not leave this Earth until you have made it a little more beautiful, a little lovelier, a little more loving.

– Osho

"What's *this* mean?" Daphne waves her essay draft impatiently, reading aloud my generic comment: "Revise for clarity."

"Well . . ." I pause and stop scanning an URGENT email from the attendance clerk. "You know, Daphne . . . make it easier for the reader to understand. Clarity. Clear."

"But what's *revise* and . . . *clarity* mean?" Daphne sighs.

"Like, make it easy for the reader to understand." I continue.

"Oh, like spelling?" Daphne's face brightens.

"Not really . . ." I sigh.

Daphne's head tilts. "So, spelling *doesn't* count then?"

"That's not exactly what I'm trying to say."

No doubt you've had similar conversations with your own writers, struggling to keep your revision hopes from dying on the vine when it all just seems so abstract.

"But how?" students plead.

There has to be a better way to teach revision. We know how you feel. We've been in similar situations, struggling to search for the right words to "get" kids to actually revise, not pretend to revise. So, in this book, we want to offer helpful, concrete, doable answers, something more than abstract generalizations, something more than a list of advice lobbed at young writers like wadded-up balls of paper:

- Revise for clarity.
- Develop this more.
- Organize your writing.
- Structure is key.
- You're all over the place. (Focus!)

Revision Truths

Longer is not always better.

Although it's true revision can make a text longer (adding detail or clarity), sometimes things need to be deleted (cut extraneous details to make writing focused to communicate an intended message).

In *Patterns of Revision*, our goal is to show how you can help your third-grade writers access these revision strategies with the tools you already have in your classroom:

- using model texts
- engaging in open-ended discussions
- reading aloud their own words
- discovering through inquiry
- learning through exploration
- playing and experimenting

Getting kids' hands and minds engaged in the act of revising is the central aim of every component of the *Patterns of Revision* process. In each lesson, we demonstrate what writers can actually *do* to revise—repeatable, practical, applicable choices, explored and named and used and evaluated. Strategies they can use anywhere in their writing regardless of genre, regardless of the assignment in front of them. Students don't always need a draft to be complete to begin incorporating these strategies. Revision is on-going.

66 Students don't always need a draft to be complete to begin incorporating these strategies. **99**

So where do we start?

It's important for students to know that we don't revise to achieve perfection. Revision isn't really about correction; it's about making sense and so much more:

- Deleting unneeded words or parts
- Rearranging sentences and paragraphs
- Adding connector words and punctuation to make relationships between and among words and ideas
- Using the power of verbs and verb forms to tighten or enhance a message
- Talking through changes and permutations to hear how they sound and better evaluate their effectiveness

Revision Truths

Shorter isn't always better either.

Though we as writers aim to be as brief as possible so that our message is heard, shorter texts aren't always complete. We want brief and effective, not skeletal and uninformative.

We opened this introduction with an epigraph that highlights the idea of "a little more." That's the way we think about revision—a process writers use to make their writing "a little more beautiful" or "a little lovelier." (We know. That's not very concrete yet—but hang on.) Our goal is to show third graders how to make their writing a little more effective and, with each experiential lesson, build a repertoire of options or choices (author's purpose and craft) that they can own and that will help them most clearly convey their meaning to their readers—or even answer multiple-choice revision test questions.

We also strive to ensure the entire learning experience around revision is "a little more loving." To that point, we're hyperaware of how revision is often talked about—and it's usually anything but loving. Do we lament or lift it? Do we malign or praise its gifts? Do we present revision as an absolute right-or-wrong proposition, or do we celebrate it as a set of powerful options that we can use as writers to effectively share our voices and communicate our passions? Because when the words fall just right, revision can inspire us with a little more awareness of options we can bring to future pieces. And this is what we want our third graders to feel. Experiences like these fortify their confidence and help them further identify as writers.

Talk It Out: The Power of Conversation to Move Writers Forward

Revision Truths

Revision isn't corrective.

Although revision makes writing better (most of the time), it isn't about fixing writing as much as it is about playing with the order, effectiveness, and clarity of words, phrases, and paragraphs. Writers revise to make sure what they write is what they mean. As always, it's about meaning and effect—not right or wrong.

We believe in the power of talk, which is why conversation is the foundation of everything in this book—the lessons, the strategies, the philosophy. Conversation is rehearsal. And since it plays such a critical role in every lesson, you'll notice speech bubbles placed as a constant reminder of the importance of talk to the *Patterns of Revision* process.

Inquiry, discovery, and interaction naturally blossom out of student talk. Talking revisions out is freeing. We are far more likely to start, stop, restart, play, and recast when we are talking instead of writing. When you make time for the joyous generation of ideas that come from talking, you build writers' revision repertoires. These conversations writers have become an internal part of their independent thinking process (Vygotsky 1978).

"But what if my kids don't talk?" you might wonder.

Third graders will talk, but they may need your help directing that talk in a productive way. Model how to talk out revision. Give them various opportunities to join in those discussions with you and each other across multiple revision lessons. Processing time is important for engagement and retention. Give writers space and grace for their conversations to unfold. Practice extending your wait time to give them a minute to start talking, and resist the ever-present urge to jump in too soon or too often to rush things along. It's better that only a little bit of natural conversation bubbles up than us trying to control it. It's their rehearsal; it's their starts and stops. Thinking can take silence, but it also needs to be unbound to allow ideas to bump against each other and take form. When we read our writing aloud or talk it out, we test our message for clarity and effectiveness. If you jump into their conversations too quickly to prompt, then students won't experience the productive struggle necessary to learn how to revise. They'll just wait for you to tell them what to revise.

Since talk is so central to the *Patterns of Revision* process and is critical in each lesson, we fold moments for talk across every chapter. That's because, in reality, the whole book's foundation is talk. To support this, we also include a full-page printable that can be used for display or for pasting in your students' notebooks (see **Talk chart**, page 14).

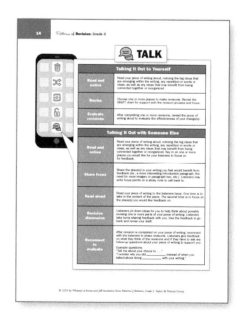

We break the DRAFT mnemonic into individual parts of the process—delete, rearrange, add connectors, and form new verbs—but it all begins and ends with talk.

Teaching the *Patterns of Revision*

The good news is that we can revise in innumerable ways: this is the beauty and freedom of revision. On the other hand, these infinite choices can also be revision's curse. Endless options can render revision overwhelming and thorny to teach—or *do*. We, our children, or any writer considering the sheer amount of revision possibilities can easily become paralyzed, frozen by trying to do it "right."

How do we help young writers decide what to do?

We expose them to options—a high-impact, specific set of revision patterns that are based upon meaning-driven decisions and the desired effect we wish to have upon our readers. We read aloud; we model. We invite students deeper into this work. They experiment and play. They share and compare. They *do*. In *Patterns of Revision*, we intend to set writers and teachers up for success. We start with literature that demonstrates what revision can do for writing. Then we invite writers to try out the *Patterns of Revision* strategy with us, with other writers, and then on their own—all while having critical discussions about the effects of our revisions.

Another way we avoid the analysis paralysis that comes with so many choices is to narrow the focus for deep study. To that end, the lessons that follow each zero in on specific doable actions, helping students realize, from the inside out, how words and the order or groupings we put them in change meaning and effect. As the lessons progress, these actions build on one another, cumulatively, to fill revisers' repertoires with options: we invite them to constantly stretch beyond what they can do now, so they can easily reach the next place.

Initially, we embolden writers to take risks and play with writing a bit at a time, with specific lessons to build their stores of options and prepare them for the cumulative work of revision. The secret of these bite-sized chunks of revision instruction is that they unlock fear by narrowing things a bit, so revision doesn't feel insurmountable or incomprehensible. Eventually, students try two, three, or four revision strategies, each grounded in a foundation of talk and integrated into the mnemonic, DRAFT, illustrated on page 5.

Tip

Talk it out! An oral test drive illuminates clumsy parts, wonderful parts, and confusing parts. Revision is talking through your writing, either internally or externally. Repeated opportunities to see the simple act of talk in play across multiple writing experiences help students develop habits for these external conversations about meaning and effect as they eventually become internal.

Revision Truths

Revision patterns do exist, and they leave writers clues for what is possible.

There are plenty of effective revision patterns writers can consider, and you can showcase them through the mnemonic DRAFT (delete, rearrange, add connectors, form new verbs, and talk it out) (see bulleted list on page 5), which Jeff included in his books *10 Things Every Writer Needs to Know* (2011) and *Revision Decisions* (2014) with Debbie Dean.

Tip

Remember, the fifth strategy of "talking it out" permeates everything we do in the *Power of Revision* process. Because it is integrated across the entire DRAFT mnemonic, we do not include a separate set of lessons for the **T** (talk it out.)

We call this the **DRAFT Reviser's Dashboard**.

- **D**elete unnecessary information
- **R**earrange
- **A**dd connectors
- **F**orm new verbs
- **T**alk it out

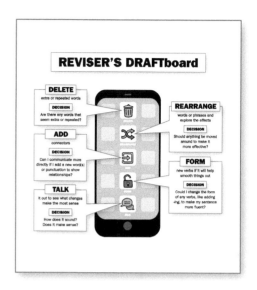

The lessons that follow are built across this mnemonic. As you work through them with your writers, remember that the lines between these options are fuzzy and naturally bleed over from one action to another. For instance, to combine sentences, or to put ideas together—an important, research-based vehicle for revision application (Graham and Perrin 2007)—writers often delete unneeded or repeated words as they rearrange sentences and ideas. Each action may, in turn, cause a cascade of new actions:

- inserting new connector punctuation such as a comma or colon
- incorporating new connector words such as conjunctions like *but, and, or, when, while, until*
- forming new verbs with different endings to compensate for deleted information or words (you need to trust us for now)
- rearranging the words or ideas to make sense

Changes force us to try exciting new possibilities, especially when we treat revision as a generative exercise of choices as we evaluate what works best at the micro- and macro-level. In this book, we introduce each revision strategy individually for deep study. But in reality, they work synergistically across the entire revision process. To that end, the last set of lessons in Part 2 extends those individual strategy lessons, looking at them collectively in what we call "combination lessons." Sentence combining uses all of our revision strategies (DRAFT) and provides meaningful practice that writers will transfer to their own work—if we are intentional.

> 66 Throughout each lesson, from start to finish and every step along the way, talking it out will play the most vital instructional role. 99

And finally, as you get started, remember this revision work is wrapped up in the power of conversations. Throughout each lesson, from start to finish and every step along the way, talking it out will play the most vital instructional role.

With all this in mind, let's explore the *Patterns of Revision* lesson structure a bit further.

Tip

Best Practice *as* Test Practice As teachers, we crave engaging and engrossing revision strategies that follow best language arts practices—conversation that raises awareness of choices and effects in mentor texts. Best practices also highlight the value of focus and clarity and most importantly tap into students' existing language pool to accelerate revision access and application. Hands-on sentence text manipulation and opportunities to talk about, apply, and discover new understandings about revision in larger applications thread through all twenty lessons included in this book. And all these conversations around effective options provide writers with the strategies they'll need on any multiple-choice or open-ended test question you put in front of them.

Patterns of Revision Lesson Overview

We love Candace Fleming's nonfiction works, and, in the example that follows, we highlight a few of her sentences from *Crash from Outer Space* (2022) to give you a helicopter view of the structure of the lessons contained in this book. After a quick instructional overview, each lesson proceeds across six components, each building on the next to encourage collective community experiences and conversations around a particular revision strategy (see Figure I.1, on page 15):

- Setting Context
- Naming the Revision Strategy
- Modeling
- Collaborating Through Conversation
- Applying Revision
- Sharing Results

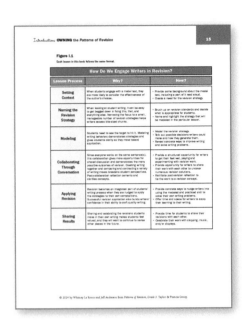

Setting the Context with Read-Aloud

In each lesson, we kick things off by setting the context. To get started, Jeff might say something like, "This is a book about the mysteries of UFOs, or unknown objects from space." Then, to further set the context, he reads aloud another section of Fleming's book:

On the evening of June 13, 1947, William "Mack" Braz sat on the porch of his tiny ranch house near Roswell, New Mexico. . . . On the horizon, a storm brewed. Bolts of jagged lightening flashed and flashed again, illuminating a mass of thick, swirling clouds. Brazel leaned forward . . . he'd never seen anything like this. The storm clouds had turned blood red and lightning kept striking the same place over and over. The thunderclaps sounded like explosions.

The sky ignited!

Throughout the past few weeks, Jeff has taken students through revision at the paragraph level—deleting, rearranging, and adding whole sentences—and now feels that his students are ready for the ultimate revision strategy: combining sentences, which takes all of his recent lessons and invites third graders to do this same work at the sentence level while thinking how ideas could be combined. He focuses on the next sentence from the read-aloud. Here is the sentence as it appears in Fleming's *Crash from Outer Space* (2022):

Like fireworks, rays of orange and red spread across the sky.

Jeff lifts this sentence and briefly makes it less effective, deconstructing it for the purposes of teaching how combining can make a piece repetitive and more concise. To that end, he untangles all of Fleming's great text. (Forgive us, Candace. Don't worry, we'll eventually share your awesome sentence, but not just yet.)

Original: Like fireworks, rays of orange and red spread across the sky.

Unrevised: It looked like there were fireworks.
They were orange.
They were red too.
The colors spread across the sky.

Naming the Revision Strategy

Jeff chooses this time after setting the context to share a specific revision strategy.

"Sometimes writing has too many words."

"Amen!" Justice says.

"When revising . . ." Jeff smiles. "One thing we can always do is use DRAFT to help us." Jeff shares the **DRAFT Reviser's Dashboard** with his students. This **DRAFT chart** is a sneak peek of the dashboard that defines the DRAFT mnemonic that students will use after they have been introduced to the strategies individually in Part 1. "So far, we've learned how to delete, rearrange, and add when we revise. Now we can do that same thing, but look a little more closely at what words are repeated that we can delete and how we might rearrange what we have left. Let's look back at Candace Fleming's writing. In her next sentence, Fleming wants to tell her reader more about the sky igniting. Let's look over her ideas and see how we might use DRAFT to revise some parts that may not work so well."

Modeling the Strategy

Jeff displays the "unrevised" version:

It looked like there were fireworks.

They were orange.

They were red too.

The colors spread across the sky.

He asks questions like "What do you notice about these four sentences? Are there any words that aren't needed or necessary for the author to get their point across? Could we take out, or delete, any words?"

As students share out their responses to his prompt, Jeff models deleting. "You've noticed that there are a few words repeated. Repetition isn't always a problem, but here I wonder if we could take out some of the repeated words."

"There are three *weres*," Xavier says.

"True," Jeff says. "Maybe we could take one or two of them out."

"There are two *theys*," Marshawn announces.

"Let's see what happens if we delete a few of these *weres* and *theys*," Jeff says.

It looked like ~~there were~~ fireworks.

They were orange.

~~They were~~ red too.

The colors spread across the sky.

"What are some ways we could rearrange or revise this? Talk to your elbow partners and think it through a bit together." After a few minutes, Jeff calls for groups to share.

Stefani begins. "You could say it looked like the fireworks were orange and red."

"Hmm!" Jeff encourages.

"That deletes, or takes out, a lot of words and still says the same thing." He sums up, "When we cut the first *were*, it caused us to note the word *there* proceeding *were* isn't needed either."

One student points to the **DRAFT chart** and notes that they'll need to add the word *and* to make their revision work. And that's just the kind of bleeding into other strategies that naturally occurs during revision, such as removing a word that no longer works, moving some things around, or adding connector words like *and* to root out repeated words.

With Jeff's guidance, the class of writers collaborates to consider what's left of the unrevised version of the model, as he challenges students to combine all four sentences remaining into one. "Have you ever started a sentence with the word *it* and somebody responded, 'What's *it*?' In general, when we write, we have to be careful when using the word *it*: we have to make clear to the audience what *it* is. Let's look at the first sentence that starts with the pronoun *it*."

It looked like ~~there were~~ fireworks.

"What is the *it* in this sentence referring to, or in other words, what's *it*?"

"I don't know!" Carlotta snaps. "*It* doesn't really say."

"Let's think about the word *it* in our sentences and to what it is referring."

It looked like ~~there were~~ fireworks.

They were orange.

~~They were~~ red too.

The colors spread across the sky.

After debating whether *it* has to do with the sky or colors, the students vote as a class. Here's what Jeff and the writers came up with:

The colors were orange and red colors spread across the sky
like fireworks.

Jeff leads a quick discussion about the effectiveness of this class-drafted version and whether there's anything they can do to improve it.

"Could we make it any better? Let's look at our **DRAFT chart** again." Jeff stares at the sentence, asking kids to reread it with him.

Jonathan jumps up. "Maybe you don't have to say the word *colors* twice."

"Ooh, deleting repeated words. That's what writers do." Jeff smiles. "Good move. Let's talk it out."

"Yeah. When you say the words *red* and *orange*, everyone already knows, they're colors, so we could just say it once: *the orange and red colors spread across the sky.*" As Vivica says this, Jeff records her words on the board and stands back.

"Yeah. Take out *the colors were,*" Sage agrees.

"How would that read?" Jeff asks. "Talk it out."

Jeff records and displays the revision as Denny talks it out, "So it would be: *The red and orange colors spread across the sky.*"

"But we can't forget about *like fireworks*! That should be in there, right?" Melissa reminds the group. Jeff stands back as the class talks it out, working together to add the phrase back into the revision.

"Good work. Do you want to see Candace Fleming's final version?" They are, in fact, dying to see it. Jeff invites the group to compare their revision with Fleming's:

Class Version: The orange and red colors spread across the sky
like fireworks.

Original Version: Like fireworks, rays of orange and red spread
across the sky.

And as students compare and contrast their sentence with Fleming's original, the group naturally starts to learn about options and choices we can make as writers. For example, sometimes when we delete, the revision needs the help of a connector sentence, word, or phrase.

"I didn't know you could use the word *like* at the beginning of a sentence!" Naomi calls from the back. Jeff smiles, knowing that this is a perfect set up for future lessons on **sentence combining** as a revision strategy.

Note, the goal here isn't matching, changing, or challenging Fleming's original; instead, we're studying it so we can think through revision possibilities and options around it, so we can learn from her brilliant process.

Collaborating Through Conversation

Next, Jeff invites the students to dive in and use conversation as a way to think about combining sentences using DRAFT in another excerpt from the same text. In groups, they work from a printable that contains another unrevised selection he's deconstructed from Fleming's book. (You can find all lesson printables and displays at the end of each lesson.)

Brazel could see the sagebrush.

Brazel could see the cacti.

He could see them clearly.

It was as if it were daytime.

Jeff begins, "Take a minute to carefully read the four sentences a couple of times with your group. Read it to yourselves and read it aloud. What do you notice?"

Students talk through the sentences and start crossing through anything that seems unneeded such as repeated words. "Work together to think through how you might reflect all of this information in one clear sentence." Once students have read through the sentences and started cutting and combining, they decide what to write down as a new version.

Student groups share their revisions with others in the class, comparing and contrasting different options and effects. Finally, after students share, Jeff invites them to look over Candace Fleming's original model sentence, continuing to explore how varying versions can accomplish more or less impactful levels of meaning.

Brazel could see the sagebrush and cacti as clearly as if it were daytime.

---

66 This exploration is very important: when we study an author's original sentence, it is not because it is the right answer but because it is an answer. This is how we learn powerful language patterns: by listening and reading other writers' work. There is no right or wrong answer; there are only options. 99

This exploration is very important: when we study an author's original sentence, it is not because it is the right answer but because it is an answer. This is how we learn powerful language patterns: by listening and reading other writers' work. There is no right or wrong answer; there are only options.

Applying Revision

Later, students will return to their own writing and look for a place where they can combine sentences or ideas. But before that, Jeff chooses to model making revisions to his own writing. So the next day, Jeff opens the class by reviewing what they've discovered so far and displays some sentences in his writer's notebook.

Adults spend tons of time worrying kids aren't happy. They don't think they're happy enough. When you do have some fun, it's always at the wrong time.

"I love to write," Jeff says. "But when I do write, if I go back and look at it later, I can usually find some ways to make it more effective. One way I can do this is to remove unnecessary ideas and sentences. First, I always look for repeated words that could be deleted. Do you see some here?"

Jamica says, "Well, it's not really repeated, but *they* and *adults* are the same thing."

"Brilliant!" He circles *adults* and *they*. "So . . . if we took out one of these words . . . someone talk out some ways we could make this into one sentence."

Students attempt to talk it out and Jeff writes down some options. Then, together, the class makes a choice of which one is the clearest and best. Afterward, Jeff concludes the discussion by inviting students to go into their notebooks or any piece of writing, old or new, and look for places they might revise some sentences and combine them using DRAFT.

Sharing Results

After they've had some time to apply the revision strategy of combining in a few of their pieces, students share and celebrate their own revisions, the *befores* and *afters*, comparing and contrasting effects and celebrating the hard work of their revisions. Jeff's goal in this sharing stage is to give young writers opportunities to hear what revising and sharing and listening to each other can do to help writers revise and to celebrate that process with students. (Another aspect of talking it out.) These repeated celebrations convince writers: "This is something I can do."

Now that we've explored its lesson structure, let's take a look at how to use this book and what's to come.

Revising at the Sentence, Paragraph, and Whole-Text Level

Every revision strategy presented in *Patterns of Revision* can be applied at the word, phrase, sentence, paragraph, or whole-text levels. For example, the lessons in Chapter 3 highlight adding in new information to help the text progress from idea to idea. We preset this concept by adding new sentences at the paragraph level, but revising by adding could happen just as surely at the sentence level, with students adding in specific words to help clarify meaning. Sometimes, writers even notice that entire pieces will need an additional paragraph to support their main point more clearly. With all this, be flexible and responsive. If you feel your writers are ready to explore adding clarifying words at the sentence level, follow that instinct. You can easily spin out from the lessons presented here to zoom in and out on these various levels of revision with your writers (see the *Patterns of Revision* **Quick List of Lesson Components**, page 16).

How to Use the *Patterns of Revision* Resource

Revision Truths

Revision requires time and thought.

One quick change isn't really revising and stretching. Revision is about making writing better, but this requires deep thought, conversation, and reflection as writers read aloud, talk things out, and explore different choices along with their effects to make sure they're saying exactly what they want their readers to understand. In short, revision is a generative activity.

This is one of those books where you *must* read the introduction. We made it short, but it's packed with information that will help you find success with *Patterns of Revision* in your classroom. Although each lesson follows the same format (see Figure I.1, page 15), this book is written in an order of progression, moving from deleting, rearranging, and adding entire sentences, phrases, or words at the paragraph level to combining ideas at the sentence level.

Part 1 lessons follow the DRAFT mnemonic revision strategies of delete, rearrange, and add in concrete, manageable bite-sized chunks, one at a time.

Part 2 builds from these to include sentence-combining lessons, which apply DRAFT in a more blended way, calling upon the revision strategies students explored in Part 1 but bringing them together in in larger contexts.

Now it's time to dive into the lessons in Chapters 1–4. Remember, they are built on talk and generation of possibilities. Make your classroom a safe place to experiment in the free flow of ideas. The lessons will help your third-grade writers reflect on purpose and effect, enhancing their abilities to revise in any setting. When choosing lessons that will best meet the needs of your students, here is a list of things to consider:

1. Read the lesson overview for each chapter. This will explain how the set of lessons differs from the others.
2. Explore the ***Patterns of Revision* Quick List of Lesson Components chart** located in Figure I.2 on page 16. This will help you zoom in on the individual lesson components while giving you an overview of how the lessons in each chapter are alike and different, as you teach the *Patterns of Revision*.
3. As you study the ***Patterns of Revision* Quick List of Lesson Components chart**, note that, with third graders, we hold off on specific lessons focused on forming new verbs and verb endings—the **F** in our DRAFT mnemonic. Because this is a level of sophistication most third graders aren't yet ready for, we fold it into the casual conversations we have during the Part 2 combining lessons, saving the explicit instruction for upper grades.

4. Each lesson will range from a minimum of forty-five minutes to an hour. Lessons could easily spill into the next day or be planned across several days. Use your discretion to adjust their pacing based on the needs of your third graders and the flexibility of your schedule.

5. Display pages and printables are included right in the lesson for which they're needed, so you can easily locate them for display or pasting into student notebooks.

6. Since the processes in this book center on talk, make sure you allow plenty of wait time after you ask questions and allow for plenty of silence after their answers to see if the students will add more. You can always sum up everything at the end.

7. You will likely find teaching the DRAFT revision strategies more manageable if you progress through the lessons in order. However, as always, we encourage you to chart a course that makes the most sense based on the needs of the student writers you work with every day.

8. As you work through the twenty lessons included in Part 1 and Part 2, recognize that they are just a starting point. They aren't intended to be comprehensive. As you develop your instructional muscles for the steps in each lesson, you'll be ready to stretch beyond them, using the structures we introduce here to plan your own *Patterns of Revision* lessons—driven by your students' ongoing needs and grounded in mentor texts your writers enjoy, celebrate, and love.

Finally, remember to have fun with your students. Play. Experiment. Talk it out. Try new ways of writing. Allow this process to grow your writing community and elevate the ways you and your students think about the power of revision.

Talking It Out to Yourself

Read and notice	Read your piece of writing aloud, noticing the big ideas that are emerging within the writing, any repetition in words or ideas, as well as any ideas that may benefit from being connected together or reorganized.
Revise	Choose one or more places to make revisions. Revisit the DRAFT chart for support with the revision process and focus.
Evaluate revisions	After completing one or more revisions, reread the piece of writing aloud to evaluate the effectiveness of your change(s).

Talking It Out with Someone Else

Read and notice	Read your piece of writing aloud, noticing the big ideas that are emerging within the writing, any repetition in words or ideas, as well as any ideas that may benefit from being connected together or reorganized. Key in on one or more places you would like for your listeners to focus on for feedback.
Share focus	Share the place(s) in your writing you feel would benefit from feedback (ex., a more interesting introduction paragraph, the need for more imagery in paragraph two, etc.). Listeners may write focus points on a sticky note to call back to.
Read aloud	Read your piece of writing to the listeners twice. One time is to take in the content of the piece. The second time is to focus on the place(s) you would like feedback on.
Revision discussion	Listeners jot down ideas for you to help think about possibly revising one or more parts of your piece of writing. Listeners take turns sharing feedback with you. Use the feedback to go back and revise your draft.
Reconnect to evaluate	After revision is completed on your piece of writing, reconnect with the listeners to share revisions. Listeners give feedback on what they think of the revisions and if they have to ask any follow-up questions about your piece of writing to support you. Example questions: "Tell me about your choice to . . ." "I wonder why you did _____ instead of when you talked about doing _____ with your writing."

Figure I.1

Each lesson in this book follows the same format.

How Do We Engage Writers in Revision?		
Lesson Process	**Why?**	**How?**
Setting Context	When students engage with a model text, they are more likely to consider the effectiveness of the author's choices.	• Provide some background about the model text, including a part of it read aloud. • Create a need for the revision strategy.
Naming the Revision Strategy	When looking at student writing, it can be easy to get bogged down in fixing this, that, and everything else. Narrowing the focus to a small, manageable number of revision strategies helps writers access bite-sized chunks.	• Brush up on revision standards and decide what is appropriate for students. • Name and highlight the strategy that will be modeled in the particular lesson.
Modeling	Students need to see the target to hit it. Modeling writing behaviors demonstrates strategies and gives students clarity as they move toward application.	• Model the revision strategy. • Talk out possible decisions writers could make and how they generate them. • Reveal concrete ways to improve writing and solve writing problems.
Collaborating Through Conversation	Since everyone works on the same sentence(s), this collaboration gives more opportunities for shared discussion and demonstrates the many possible outcomes of revision. Creating writing together and comparing and contrasting a variety of writing moves broadens student perspectives. Post-collaboration reflection cements and clarifies concepts.	• Provide a structured opportunity for writers to get their feet wet, playing and experimenting with revision work. • Provide opportunity for writers to share their work with each other to uncover numerous revision solutions. • Facilitate post-revision reflection to tie the work to a revision concept.
Applying Revision	Revision becomes an integrated part of students' writing process when they are nudged to apply the strategies to their own compositions. Successful revision application also builds writers' confidence in their ability to craft quality writing.	• Provide concrete ways to nudge writers into using the modeled and practiced skill to solve their own writing problems. • Offer time and space for writers to apply their learning to their writing.
Sharing Results	Sharing and celebrating the revisions students make in their own writing makes students feel valued, and they will want to continue to revise other pieces in the future.	• Provide time for students to share their revisions with each other. • Celebrate their work with clapping, music, and/or displays.

Figure I.2

Patterns of Revision Quick List of Lesson Components						
Lesson Sets	**Part 1** (Pages 21 – 123)					**Part 2** (Pages 125 – 246)
Revision Strategies	**Delete**	**Rearrange**	**Add Connectors**	**Form new verbs**	**Talk**	**Combining**
Setting the Context	Identify and lift an engaging piece of authentic writing to serve as a model. Introduce the model excerpt to writers, giving some background information and building interest.	Identify and lift an engaging piece of authentic writing to serve as a model. Introduce the model excerpt to writers, giving some background information and building interest.	Identify and lift an engaging piece of authentic writing to serve as a model. Introduce the model excerpt to writers, giving some background information and building interest.	In the Grade 3 resource, we make room for the fact that **forming new verbs or verb endings** may be a bit daunting for third graders.	Conversation is so key that we introduce "**talking it out**" early in the introduction of *Patterns of Revision* and fold it into every lesson of this book.	Part II pulls the thread of **DRAFT** through the rest of the lessons, weaving in strategies from all the lessons and conversations that have come before. As always, the lessons in this set start with lifting and introducing an engaging piece of authentic writing for study and discussion.
Naming the Revision Strategy	Establish and define **deleting** as a powerful revision strategy, naming it as the purpose for the lesson with a continued focus on the model text.	Establish and define **rearranging** as a powerful revision strategy, naming it as the purpose for the lesson with a continued focus on the model text.	Establish and define **adding connectors** as a powerful revision strategy, naming it as the purpose for the lesson with a continued focus on the model text.	While the strategy is important, we've chosen to integrate this more difficult concept conversationally, highlighting it briefly in Part II through sentence combining.		Name that revisers ultimately use all the **DRAFT** strategies and note how some decisions prompt additional choices that need to be made. Emphasize this strategy is about finding a combination that works. There is no one right answer.
Modeling the Strategy	Demonstrate the power of **deleting unneeded or repetitive sentences, words, or phrases**, studying the choices the author of the model text made, talking, thinking, creating, and sharing.	Demonstrate the power of **rearranging words and sentences to help make our writing more organized and structured**, studying the choices the author of the model text made, talking, thinking, creating, and sharing.	Demonstrate the power of **adding connector sentences, words, and punctuation to help make writing easy to follow**, studying the choices the author of the model text made, talking, thinking, creating, and sharing.	We expand on the sophisticated strategy of **forming new verbs/ verb endings** with greater detail in subsequent Patterns of Revision resources for grades 4–8.		Demonstrate **combining multiple strategies** in one revising event— reading through options, referring back to the DRAFT mnemonic, making critical decisions, and talking them out while continually considering meaning and effectiveness.

Figure I.2 *(continued)*

Patterns of Revision Quick List of Lesson Components						
Lesson Sets	**Part 1** (Pages 21 – 123)					**Part 2** (Pages 125 – 246)
Revision Strategies	**Delete**	**Rearrange**	**Add Connectors**	**Form new verbs**	**Talk**	**Combining**
Collaborating Through Conversation	Working together and using a new text excerpt, writers talk through possibilities for **deleting unnecessary or repetitive, sentences, words, or phrases.**	Working together and using a new text excerpt, writers talk through revision possibilities, **rearranging and moving sentences around and reorganizing them** to see what effect it has on the reader.	Working together and using a new text excerpt, writers talk through possibilities for **adding in new information, sentences, words, or phrases** to connect ideas in a clear way.	In the Grade 3 resource, we make room for the fact that **forming new verbs or verb endings** may be a bit daunting for third graders.\n\nWhile the strategy is important, we've chosen to integrate this more difficult concept conversationally, highlighting it briefly in Part II through sentence combining.\n\nWe expand on the sophisticated strategy of **forming new verbs/ verb endings** with greater detail in subsequent Patterns of Revision resources for grades 4–8.	Conversation is so key that we introduce **"talking it out"** early in the introduction of *Patterns of Revision* and fold it into every lesson of this book.	Working together and using a new text excerpt, revisers think through possibilities for **combining multiple sentences into one** while calling back to previously learned revision strategies (DRAFT), trying them out, talking them through, and using all this to Make effective, meaning-centered revision decisions.
Applying Revision	Writers try out the strategy in their own writing by returning to previous drafts or pieces from their writing notebooks to revise using the power of **deleting** to make their writing effective, talking through options either internally or with peers.	Writers try out the strategy in their own writing by returning to previous drafts or pieces from their writing notebooks to revise using the power of **rearranging** to make their writing effective, talking through options either internally or with peers.	Writers try out the strategy in their own writing by returning to previous drafts or pieces from their writing notebooks to revise using the power of **adding connectors** to make writing easier to follow talking through options either internally or with peers.			Revisers try out **combining** strategies in their own writing by returning to previous drafts or pieces from their writing notebooks. They revise using a **combination of all or a collection of the DRAFT revision strategies** —deleting, rearranging, adding, forming new verbs, and, of course, talking it out either internally or with peers.
Sharing Results	Writers share and celebrate by reading aloud from their new pieces while revisiting the newly learned revision strategy and talking through how their choices to **delete unnecessary sentences, phrases, or words** affect meaning and make their pieces stronger.	Writers share and celebrate by reading aloud from their new pieces while revisiting the newly learned revision strategy and talking through how their choices to **rearrange sentences, phrases, or words** affect meaning and make their pieces stronger.	Writers share and celebrate by reading aloud from their new pieces while revisiting the newly learned revision strategy and talking through how their choices to **add new details to connect** affect meaning and make their pieces stronger.			Revisers share and celebrate by reading aloud from their new pieces while talking through the individual **DRAFT revision strategies** they considered and how their ultimate decisions enhance their message and make their piece stronger.\n\nAs always, steer this conversation toward choice and effect. There isn't one right answer.

Connecting the *Patterns of Revision* to the *Patterns of Power*

If you've come to this book by way of our previous work in the *Patterns of Power* series, this book is not intended as a replacement but rather a supplement to that family of resources. *Patterns of Power* focuses on studying authors' use of grammar and mechanics to create meaning and effect. *Patterns of Revision* can easily be used in concert with the ongoing work you're doing with grammar instruction—or its lessons can stand on their own. As in *Patterns of Power*, the carefully orchestrated lessons in this book provide all you need, including curated excerpts from authentic literature and culturally nourishing texts (Qarooni 2024) to spark powerful revision conversations along with twenty lesson plans with correlating printables, displays, and step-by-step visual instructions to generate engaging experiences to make revising with depth accessible and memorable to third graders.

Patterns of Revision Lesson	Lesson Type	Goal Focus	Mentor Text Title	Patterns of Power, Grades 1–5 Connection
3.1 Does This Belong Here?	Delete	Delete unnecessary or repetitive information that obscures meaning.	*Darryl's Dream*	
3.2 *Turtle*-ly Unnecessary	Delete	Delete unnecessary information that obscures meaning within a sequential structure.	*Follow the Moon Home: A Tale of One Idea, Twenty Kids, and a Hundred Sea Turtles*	*PoP* Lesson 11.2 Everyday Agreement: Nouns and Verbs
3.3 Line Tamer	Delete	Delete unnecessary information that obscures meaning within a question-answer structure.	*The Lion Queens of India*	
3.4 Rearranger in Time	Rearrange	Rearrange ideas and sentences to ensure a logical progression.	*Ranger in Time: Disaster on the Titanic*	
3.5 Sorting Sentences	Rearrange	Rearrange ideas and sentences with time-order words to ensure a logical progression within a sequential structure.	*Billy Miller Makes a Wish*	
3.6 Take Action and Rearrange	Rearrange	Rearrange ideas and sentences to ensure a logical progression focusing on main idea and details.	*Stand Up! 10 Mighty Women Who Made a Change*	

(continued)

Patterns of Revision Lesson	Lesson Type	Goal Focus	Mentor Text Title	Patterns of Power, Grades 1–5 Connection
3.7 **Like Gecko Feet: Clarifying Information Keeps Your Writing Together**	Add	Add sentences to clarify for the reader.	*Mimic Makers: Biomimicry Inventors Inspired by Nature*	
3.8 **Take the Liberty to Add Connecting Sentences**	Add	Add a sentence to connect one idea to the next, giving the piece coherence.	*Let Liberty Rise! How America's Schoolchildren Helped Save the Statue of Liberty*	*PoP* Lesson 13.3 Ink a Link: Using Adjectives After the Verb
3.9 **Cat Got Your Transition?**	Add	Connect ideas by adding precise words, phrases, and transitions.	*The Cat Man of Aleppo*	*PoP* Lesson 15.3 Sooner or Later: Adverbs of Time
3.10 **The Art and Architecture of DRAFT**	Combine	Combine ideas to avoid redundancy, add clarity, and improve fluency: a list using the serial comma.	*Dream Builder: The Story of Architect Philip Freelon*	*PoP* Lesson 19.1 Catalog a Frog: Items in a List *PoP* Lesson 19.2 Whatever Rings Your Smell: Items in a List
3.11 **Drawing Things Together**	Combine	Combine ideas to avoid redundancy, add clarity, and improve fluency: compound predicate and adverbs that tell time.	*Drawing on Walls: A Story of Keith Haring*	*PoP* Lesson 15.3 Sooner or Later: Adverbs of Time *PoP* Lesson 19.3 Sisters, Brothers, or Friends: A Series of Things They Do
3.12 **Dinner Time**	Combine	Combine ideas to avoid redundancy, add clarity, and improve fluency: future tense and placement of prepositional phrases.	*A Different Pond*	*PoP* Lesson 16.1 A Phrase I'm Going Through: PrePOSITIONS *PoP* Lesson 16.2 You Rang? When and Where? *PoP* Lesson 16.3 One Prepared Pig: Which One? *PoP* Lesson 6.3 Have You Got the Time? Verb Tense
3.13 **There's More to Hair Than Meets Eye**	Combine	Combine ideas to avoid redundancy, add clarity, and improve fluency: compound predicate.	*J.D. and the Great Barber Battle*	
3.14 **Read the Room**	Combine	Combine ideas to avoid redundancy, add clarity, and improve fluency: show possession.	*Yasmin the Librarian*	*PoP* Lesson 9.1 Let's Eat: Apostrophes of Restaurant Ownership *PoP* Lesson 9.2 Apostrophe Family Reunion: Contractions and Possessives

(continues)

(continued)

Patterns of Revision Lesson	Lesson Type	Goal Focus	Mentor Text Title	Patterns of Power, Grades 1–5 Connection
3.15 Everything in Its Place	Combine	Combine ideas to avoid redundancy, add clarity, and improve fluency: descriptive word choice.	*Lia Park and the Missing Jewel*	
3.16 Putting Sentences Together, One by One	Combine	Combine ideas to avoid redundancy, add clarity, and improve fluency: compound subjects and compound predicates.	*Rise Up and Write It*	
3.17 Combining Forces: The Butterfly Effect	Combine	Combine ideas to avoid redundancy, add clarity, and improve fluency: series of actions and beginning sentence with an opener.	*Butterfly for a King: Saving Hawaii's Kamehameha Butterflies*	*PoP* Lesson 6.1 Verbs Move: Verbs Mean Action
3.18 Combine to Make Ideas Bloom	Combine	Combine ideas to avoid redundancy, add clarity, and improve fluency: infinitive verbs.	*What's Inside a Flower? And Other Questions About Science and Nature*	
3.19 Dreaming of Better Sentences	Combine	Combine ideas to avoid redundancy, add clarity, and improve fluency: compound sentences.	*Barefoot Dreams of Petra Luna*	*PoP* Lesson 18.1 Curious and Studied: Combining Sentences *PoP* Lesson 18.3 The Draw of a Compound Sentence: Coordinating Contrast *PoP* Lesson 18.4 So . . . : What Compound Sentences Cause and Effect
3.20 Sentence Combining Is a Slam Dunk	Combine	Combine ideas to avoid redundancy, add clarity, and improve fluency: complex sentences.	*Above the Rim: How Elgin Baylor Changed Basketball*	*PoP* Lesson 20.1 *If* You Give a Writer a Model: The Conditional Subordinate *PoP* Lesson 20.2 AAAWWUBBIS: From Garbage to Treasure *PoP* Lesson 20.3 Robot AAAWWUBBIS: As You Know *PoP* Lesson 20.4 Before You Lose Your Nerve: AAAWWUBBIS Continued *PoP* Lesson 20.5 Plenty of Raisins for No Comma: When AAAWWUBBIS Isn't First

Part 1

EXPLORING

Patterns

of

REVISION

in

Bite-Sized

CHUNKS

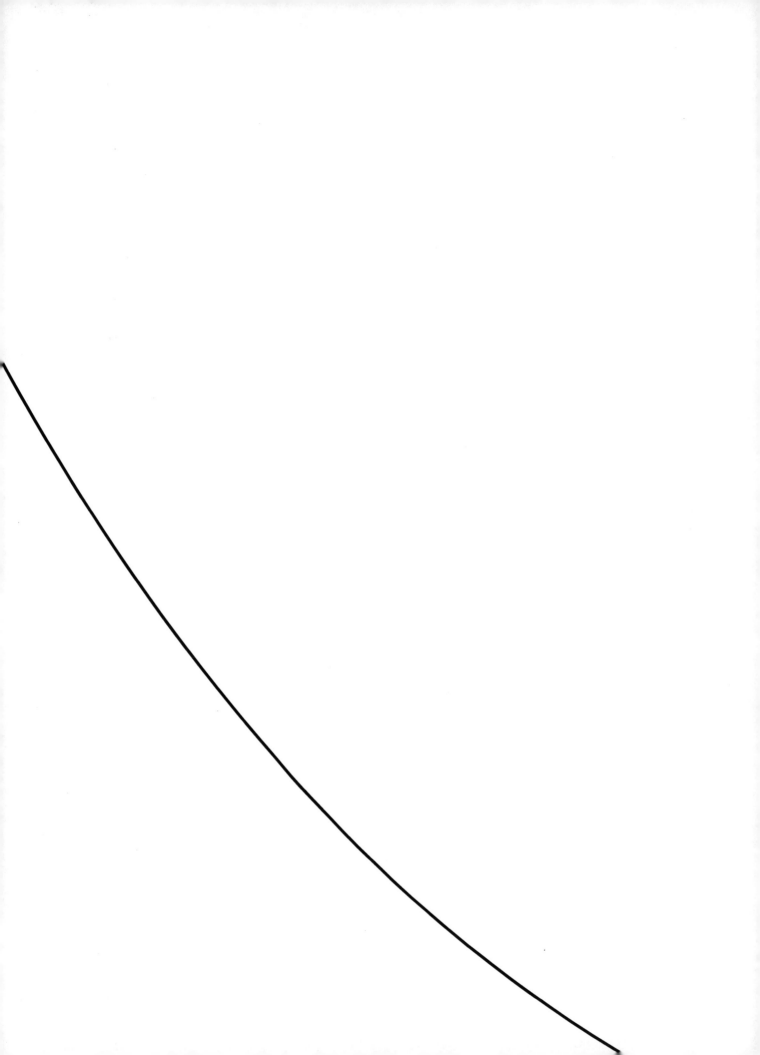

1

Invitation to
DELETE UNNECESSARY INFORMATION

Getting rid of clutter gives writing its due space: space for thought, space for readers to soak in what's important, space for what matters most. When we clear out the clutter, our best thoughts surface and shine.

– Jeff Anderson, *10 Things Every Writer Needs to Know*

We like to ground the lessons in this chapter's set with an initial exploration of the word *necessary*, asking students to share out what it means. Invariably someone will say something like, "You *have* to do something."

"So, if something is necessary, you *have* to do it. It's important. It's needed. Now think about the prefix *-un*. Turn to your neighbor and discuss what the prefix *-un* usually does to a word when attached to the beginning of it." The discussion usually produces some responses like "*-Un* almost always means *not*" or "*-Un* can mean 'the opposite of.'"

Then, we ask them to consider how adding *-un* to the beginning of the word *necessary* changes the meaning. We discuss how the opposite of necessary means something you don't need or have to do. Now we're cooking with gas.

In this chapter, we include three starter lessons to help students begin to think about parts of their writing that are unnecessary—inclusions they don't need because they're ineffective, places where things are repetitive, or things they don't have to have for their piece to make sense.

As you lead your writers through the work of deleting words, phrases, and sentences presented across this chapter, your conversations may naturally evolve to include the idea that revisers can also choose to delete larger chunks of text like whole paragraphs. For specific guidance in extending discussions with your writers beyond these lessons to the paragraph level, see the **Delete chart** on page 24. Students may keep a copy of this chart in their writing folder, glue a copy into their writing notebook, or access a copy hanging in your classroom.

All of the lessons in this chapter follow a similar format. We include a sentence with extra information that *doesn't belong* in the paragraph, and then we invite students to consider which sentence should be deleted and why. First, we try one out together, then writers try a different one in small groups or with partners. To conclude the lesson, students return to their own writing to delete unnecessary details, sentences, or words that get in the way of meaning for readers. We learn by doing, so let's start deleting.

> 66 In this chapter, we include three starter lessons to help students begin to think about parts of their writing that are unnecessary—inclusions they don't need because they're ineffective, places where things are repetitive, or things they don't have to have for their piece to make sense. 99

DELETE

Deleting at the **Sentence** Level

Get rid of **WORDY WORDS**
(words that don't say much or are repetitive)

Check your writing for word pairs that actually do the same thing. Delete the extra word.

Examples:

fall down	**BECOMES**	fall
past history	**BECOMES**	past
unexpected surprise	**BECOMES**	surprise
cancel out	**BECOMES**	cancel

Use a single word to say the same thing as the pair or group of words.

Examples:

said loudly	**BECOMES**	yelled
at the present time	**BECOMES**	now

If you are looking to cut words that don't do much work, check your writing for some of the words below. They don't always need to be deleted, but can be easily removed without affecting meaning.

Examples:

absolutely	quite
all	really
completely	sort of
definitely	totally
just	very
kind of	would

Deleting at the **Paragraph** Level

Find your focus
- Read or reread one paragraph you wrote.
- Think about and decide what you think is the main topic or focus of the paragraph.
- Write or say the main focus of the paragraph in one word, phrase, or sentence.

Check your writing for extra ideas not related to your main focus
- After deciding on a main focus, reread your paragraph. Are there any parts of the paragraph that don't match your focus?
- If not, move on to looking at the next paragraph of your composition.
- If so, you have some choices to make:
  - Move these extra ideas somewhere else, either connected to another paragraph or into a new paragraph or another piece of future writing.
  - If these ideas don't fit anywhere, delete them.

3.1 Does this Belong Here?

Lesson Overview

Revision goal connected to standards:

Develop and strengthen writing by deleting unnecessary or repetitive information that obscures meaning.

Model Text

Darryl's Dream
- Written by Darryl "DMC" McDaniels with Shawnee and Johnny Warfield and Adam Padilla
- Illustrated by Tristan Tait

Teacher Considerations

One of the hardest revision skills for young writers is deleting information. When revising, we ask writers to identify places in their writing that may seem unclear to the readers, but often the reason a piece is unclear is because it includes repetitive information, and this extraneous writing ends up creating distractive clutter. To help them gain confidence in deleting information that doesn't belong, we invite writers to approach revision with conversations and thinking around meaning and effect, instead of what's right and what's wrong. Although deleting unnecessary or repetitive information is a strategy writers use across all genres, we showcase different genres in this chapter. *Darryl's Dream* is a narrative story, told in third-person point of view, that also includes a poem in the form of a rap song, referred to within the story, at the end of the book. Even though our focus with this lesson is on deleting a sentence that doesn't belong because it demonstrates repetition, the selection is also powerfully descriptive, so you could revisit this model when students are working on using descriptive details in their writing.

Since this will likely be the first *Patterns of Revision* lesson you provide for your students, you may choose to add more guidance during the discussion. If you do, be sure to leave ample time for authentic conversation, keeping this lesson focused on your students' thoughts and discoveries rather than a checklist of tasks.

Setting the Context

Based on the true story of hip-hop pioneer Darryl "DMC" McDaniel, *Darryl's Dream* shares a message to be true to yourself and confident in who you are, even when others treat you poorly. Read aloud the excerpt in which the main character, Darryl, has a dream about seeing himself as a star in a music recording studio. *Shh.* We've added a sentence that repeats information and doesn't belong, but don't tell your students that. You'll reveal the original version later.

> Suddenly, Darryl found himself inside a recording studio. Darryl was in a recording studio with fancy equipment. There were instruments everywhere, and there was lots of fancy equipment. The walls were lined with gold records. Darryl looked at one of the awards and saw . . . himself!

Prompt your students with "Sometimes when we write, we include information that doesn't really belong, or we say the same thing over and over again as we try to add details. This can be confusing for our readers. Do you feel like there is some information that doesn't belong or says the same thing—like it repeats information?"

 Revision Strategy

Delete unnecessary or repetitive information.

Modeling

Display **3.1 Unnecessary Sentence: Part I**, which includes each sentence from the model excerpt (and a repetitive sentence that needs to be deleted) numbered in order. For students who could benefit from physically manipulating them, you may choose to display the individual sentences on index cards or sentence strips—or even electronically.

To spark some thinking around deleting unnecessary or repetitive information, ask students, "What is this paragraph mostly about?" Then guide your students through a discussion about choosing which sentence doesn't really belong and why. "Something is off in this paragraph. Let's check each sentence, one by one, to see if it ties back to the big idea of this paragraph." Think aloud while modeling how to reread, taking out a different sentence each time and talking the change through to examine its effect on meaning. Students will likely notice that some of the information is repeated.

Students talk it out for each sentence using the following questions to prompt the conversation:

- How would deleting this sentence affect the meaning? WHY?
- Do we need this sentence? WHY or WHY NOT?

Through discussion, help students consider how sentence #2 doesn't belong because it repeats the information in both sentence #1 and sentence #3. It's extra. Display **3.1 Unnecessary Sentence: Part II** to reveal the original excerpt from *Daryl's Dream* and compare how the different version affects meaning.

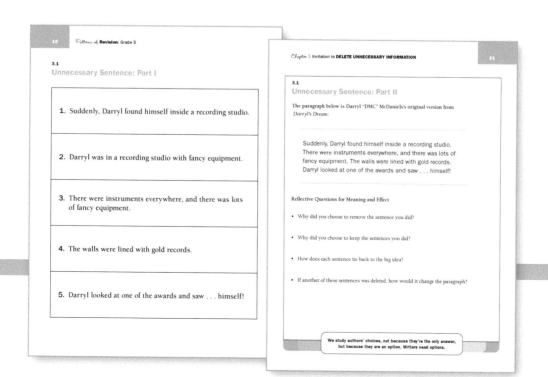

Collaborating Through Conversation

Organize students into pairs or small groups. Display the sentences lifted from **3.1 Invitation to Delete: Part I** (e.g., on index cards or sentence strips or electronically). In pairs or small groups, students collaborate through conversation to order the sentences in a way that makes sense and tightly connects the ideas. When ready, students compare their order with others in class and share why they chose the order they did. Following the directions on the display, students collaborate through conversation to delete the unnecessary sentence. To help students talk it out, remind them to explore how each sentence supports or ties into the main idea or message of the paragraph and to look for information that may be repeated. By justifying their thinking, students take ownership of their decision to delete.

When ready, students compare their deletion choice with others in class, talking through their decisions together. The point here is for them to discuss WHY they made the choice. Display **3.1 Invitation to Delete: Part II** to share the author's original text for comparative analysis, using the reflective questions to facilitate a conversation about meaning and effect.

Applying Revision

Students return to their own writing or their writer's notebook and play with deleting unnecessary or repetitive information while gauging the effects of such removals (Figure 3.1). To help them focus, encourage writers to choose one section or paragraph to revise at a time. Some students may find it helpful to write each sentence on a strip of paper, so they can physically manipulate their writing, deciding if each sentence connects to the meaning of the piece. It may help students to talk it out with a partner or in their heads as they consider their own big ideas against information that is needed and not needed. Some students may decide nothing needs to be deleted. In this case, encourage them to move on to other sections of their pieces and continue the process. You can also invite them to consider repetitive words. Sometimes writers decide to delete only a word or phrase that is repetitive, too. Writers have options.

Figure 3.1

A third grader deletes repetitive or unnecessary information from his draft about football.

Sharing Results

Writers share their revisions with others and celebrate their work by naming how their revisions will help their readers understand their writing more clearly. Some students may have chosen to delete a few words or phrases while others deleted entire sentences, or even paragraphs. Provide positive feedback by pointing out—or inviting them to point out—how their revisions helped the reader.

3.1
Unnecessary Sentence: Part I

1. Suddenly, Darryl found himself inside a recording studio.

2. Darryl was in a recording studio with fancy equipment.

3. There were instruments everywhere, and there was lots of fancy equipment.

4. The walls were lined with gold records.

5. Darryl looked at one of the awards and saw . . . himself!

3.1

Unnecessary Sentence: Part II

The paragraph below is Darryl "DMC" McDaniels's original version from
Darryl's Dream:

Suddenly, Darryl found himself inside a recording studio.
There were instruments everywhere, and there was lots of
fancy equipment. The walls were lined with gold records.
Darryl looked at one of the awards and saw . . . himself!

Reflective Questions for Meaning and Effect

- Why did you choose to remove the sentence you did?

- Why did you choose to keep the sentences you did?

- How does each sentence tie back to the big idea?

- If another of these sentences was deleted, how would it change the paragraph?

We study authors' choices, not because they're the only answer,
but because they are an option. Writers need options.

3.1

Invitation to Delete: Part I

> In the following excerpt from Darryl "DMC" McDaniels's *Darryl's Dream*, the main character, Darryl, is about to share his poetry during the school's talent show.

- Read the paragraph first. What is it mostly about?

- Talk it out as you decide which sentence provides unnecessary or repetitive information and remove it.

- When you finish, read the passage aloud to your group to see if it now flows smoothly.

- Compare your version with other groups or pairs in your class.

- Compare your version with the author's original text.

3.1

Invitation to Delete: Part I *(continued)*

1. That afternoon, it was time for the talent show.

2. Darryl waited backstage for his cue.

3. He put on a new hat, pushed up his glasses, and held on to his poem.

4. He was going to read his poem at the talent show.

5. He was very nervous.

3.1

Invitation to Delete: Part II

The paragraph below shows Darryl "DMC" McDaniels's choices as a writer in *Darryl's Dream*:

That afternoon, it was time for the talent show. Darryl waited backstage for his cue. He put on a new hat, pushed up his glasses, and held on to his poem. He was very nervous.

Reflective Questions for Meaning and Effect

- Why did you choose to remove the sentence you did?

- Why did you choose to keep the sentences you did?

- How does each sentence tie back to the big idea?

- If another sentence was deleted, how would it change the paragraph?

> **We study authors' choices, not because they're the only answer, but because they are an option. Writers need options.**

3.2 *Turtle*-ly Unnecessary

Lesson Overview

Revision goal connected to standards:

Develop and strengthen writing by deleting unnecessary information that obscures meaning.

Model Text

Follow the Moon Home: A Tale of One Idea, Twenty Kids, and a Hundred Sea Turtles
  – Written by Philippe Cousteau and Deborah Hopkison
  – Illustrated by Meilo So

Teacher Considerations

With this lesson, we continue to invite our writers into conversations about meaning and effect as they think about what information belongs and what information could be deleted. We add a sentence that is unnecessary and doesn't support the rest of the selection. Since revising is a flexible process, we remind our students to cross out the deleted information, rather than erase, so they see that it is gone for now, but it doesn't have to remain permanently deleted. They may eventually find a better place for that information somewhere else in their piece, or another one.

   The narrative text we chose for this lesson, *Follow the Moon Home: A Tale of One Idea, Twenty Kids, and a Hundred Sea Turtles* by Philippe Cousteau and Deborah Hopkison, uses words and phrases to show when, helping the reader step through the text in a sequential order.

Patterns of Power Lesson 11.2: Everyday Agreement: Nouns and Verbs may focus on subject-verb agreement across four sentences, but it's a nice tie-in to this revision lesson as well, inviting considerations why the information in the four sentences belongs and how they are connected.

Setting the Context

Philippe Cousteau and Deborah Hopkinson's *Follow the Moon Home: A Tale of One Idea, Twenty Kids, and a Hundred Sea Turtles* shares a story of how young people can impact change in their community and protect their environment. To set the context, read aloud the excerpt in which the main character, Viv, explains how her class's mission to save the loggerhead sea turtle hatchlings began. Keep in mind that we've added a sentence that doesn't belong, but don't tell your students that. You'll reveal the original version later.

On Monday morning, Clementine and I raised our hands first. We told the class what we'd learned and observed about loggerhead sea turtles. I always need help finding my way, especially in a new place. "The sea turtle eggs are starting to hatch," I went on. "To save the hatchlings we need the whole class—the whole town—to help." And that's how *Lights Out for Loggerheads* began.

Prompt your students with, "Sometimes when we write, we include information that doesn't really support our message and can confuse our readers. Is this paragraph coherent, with all ideas tightly connected, or do you feel like maybe there is some information that doesn't really belong?"

 **Revision Strategy**
Delete unnecessary information.

Modeling

Display **3.2 Unnecessary Sentence: Part I**, which includes each sentence from the model excerpt (and an unnecessary sentence that needs to be deleted) numbered in order. For students who could benefit from physically manipulating them, you may choose to display the individual sentences on index cards or sentence strips—or even electronically.

To invite the thinking that is involved in deleting unnecessary information, ask students, "What is this paragraph mostly about?" Then share with your students that one of the sentences in this paragraph does not support this big idea. "Something is off in this paragraph. Let's check each sentence, one by one, to see if it ties back to what the paragraph is mostly about, what was happening in class Viv's class that day." Think aloud while modeling how to remove a sentence, reread, and examine its effect on meaning.

Continue to model this process with the sentences, and invite your students to talk it out for each one, prompting the conversation as needed:

- How would deleting this sentence affect the meaning? WHY?
- Do we need this sentence? WHY or WHY NOT?

Through discussion, the students consider how sentence #3 doesn't belong because it is not about explaining the issue of the sea turtle hatchlings to the class and the need to help them. It doesn't belong here, but it could go somewhere else in the piece. Explain that in our own writing, we would simply cross it out with one line, in case we change our mind or find another place for it later.

Use the display page, **3.2 Unnecessary Sentence: Part II**, to reveal the original excerpt from *Follow the Moon Home: A Tale of One Idea, Twenty Kids, and a Hundred Sea Turtles* and compare how the original version affects meaning.

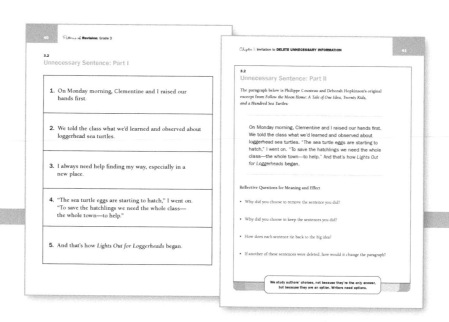

Collaborating Through Conversation

Display **3.2 Invitation to Delete: Part I**. In pairs or small groups, students collaborate through conversation to delete the sentence they think is not needed. To help students talk it out, remind them to explore how each sentence supports or ties into what the paragraph is mostly about. By justifying their thinking, students take ownership of their decision to delete.

When ready, students compare their deletion choice with others in class, sharing WHY they made the choice. Using the display page **3.2 Invitation to Delete: Part II**, share the authors' original text for comparative analysis, using its reflective questions to facilitate a conversation about meaning and effect.

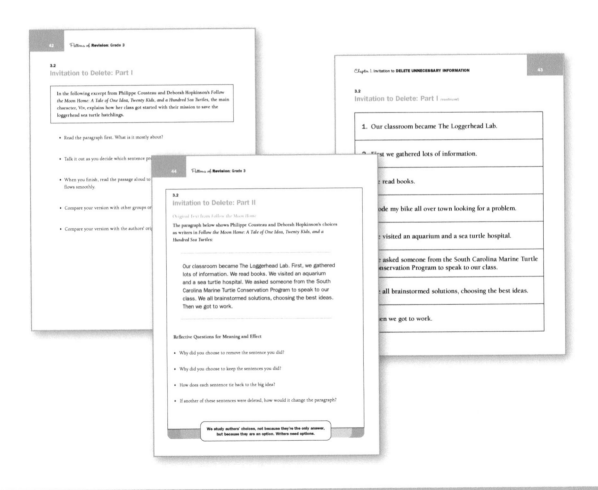

Applying Revision

Students return to their own writing and choose a small three- to four-sentence part of a previously drafted piece to focus on and draw a box around it. Remind them to first think, "What is this boxed part mostly about?" It may help to write this big idea on a sticky note and place it on the draft outside of their box. Then, they read through each sentence, checking to see if it is connected to the big idea or not. If it doesn't really belong, they draw a line through it to show it doesn't go there, but maybe it will end up somewhere else. It may help students to talk it out with a partner as they consider what information is needed and not needed. If time permits, students choose another part to box out and study, or even take a look at the piece in its entirety, making sure each sentence within the piece connects tightly to the big idea. If they happen to find a better place for any of their deleted sentences, they can insert it where it belongs. Revision is ongoing.

Sharing Results

Celebrate the messy work of revision by inviting students to show others where they deleted information. Consider taking your students to another class, perhaps in a different grade level, to act as mentors for revision, sharing what parts of their pieces they decided to take out and why. Hold on to their revised drafts after they have published, and hang this messy work in the hallway next to their published pieces to showcase the process of revision.

3.2

Unnecessary Sentence: Part I

1. On Monday morning, Clementine and I raised our hands first.

2. We told the class what we'd learned and observed about loggerhead sea turtles.

3. I always need help finding my way, especially in a new place.

4. "The sea turtle eggs are starting to hatch," I went on. "To save the hatchlings we need the whole class— the whole town—to help."

5. And that's how *Lights Out for Loggerheads* began.

3.2

Unnecessary Sentence: Part II

The paragraph below is Philippe Cousteau and Deborah Hopkinson's original excerpt from *Follow the Moon Home: A Tale of One Idea, Twenty Kids, and a Hundred Sea Turtles*:

On Monday morning, Clementine and I raised our hands first. We told the class what we'd learned and observed about loggerhead sea turtles. "The sea turtle eggs are starting to hatch," I went on. "To save the hatchlings we need the whole class—the whole town—to help." And that's how *Lights Out for Loggerheads* began.

Reflective Questions for Meaning and Effect

- Why did you choose to remove the sentence you did?

- Why did you choose to keep the sentences you did?

- How does each sentence tie back to the big idea?

- If another of these sentences were deleted, how would it change the paragraph?

> **We study authors' choices, not because they're the only answer, but because they are an option. Writers need options.**

3.2
Invitation to Delete: Part I

In the following excerpt from Philippe Cousteau and Deborah Hopkinson's *Follow the Moon Home: A Tale of One Idea, Twenty Kids, and a Hundred Sea Turtles*, the main character, Viv, explains how her class got started with their mission to save the loggerhead sea turtle hatchlings.

- Read the paragraph first. What is it mostly about?

- Talk it out as you decide which sentence provides unnecessary information.

- When you finish, read the passage aloud to your group to see if it now flows smoothly.

- Compare your version with other groups or pairs in your class.

- Compare your version with the authors' original text.

3.2

Invitation to Delete: Part I *(continued)*

1. Our classroom became The Loggerhead Lab.

2. First we gathered lots of information.

3. We read books.

4. I rode my bike all over town looking for a problem.

5. We visited an aquarium and a sea turtle hospital.

6. We asked someone from the South Carolina Marine Turtle Conservation Program to speak to our class.

7. We all brainstormed solutions, choosing the best ideas.

8. Then we got to work.

3.2

Invitation to Delete: Part II

Original Text from *Follow the Moon Home*

The paragraph below shows Philippe Cousteau and Deborah Hopkinson's choices as writers in *Follow the Moon Home: A Tale of One Idea, Twenty Kids, and a Hundred Sea Turtles*:

Our classroom became The Loggerhead Lab. First, we gathered lots of information. We read books. We visited an aquarium and a sea turtle hospital. We asked someone from the South Carolina Marine Turtle Conservation Program to speak to our class. We all brainstormed solutions, choosing the best ideas. Then we got to work.

Reflective Questions for Meaning and Effect

• Why did you choose to remove the sentence you did?

• Why did you choose to keep the sentences you did?

• How does each sentence tie back to the big idea?

• If another of these sentences were deleted, how would it change the paragraph?

We study authors' choices, not because they're the only answer, but because they are an option. Writers need options.

3.3 Line Tamer

Lesson Overview

Revision goal connected to standards:

Develop and strengthen writing by deleting unnecessary information that obscures meaning.

Model Text

The Lion Queens of India
- — Written by Jan Reynolds

Teacher Considerations

With this lesson, we use a nonfiction text written in first-person point of view to continue to engage students in conversations about meaning and effect as they think about what information belongs and what information could be deleted. We also like this text as a mentor for young writers because it concludes with a structure that opens with a question followed by an essay response much like the prompt-based writing our students are often asked to do for assessments.

We begin this lesson with the specific question asked toward the end of *The Lion Queens of India* by Jan Reynolds, and we invite our students to consider how the paragraph answers the question, what information is needed to answer the question, and what information is extra.

Setting the Context

To set the context, read aloud the excerpt of Jan Reynolds's *The Lion Queens of India* in which the Lion Queen, Rashila, who helps to take care of the lions of India, begins to answer the question: How can humans and animals both thrive, living near each other and competing for the same resources? *Shh*. We've added a sentence that doesn't belong, but don't tell your students that. You'll reveal the original version later.

How can humans and animals both thrive, living near each other and competing for the same resources?

To address this question, we Lion Queens work with the communities surrounding Gir to teach them about the lions' needs and behavior. Visitors to the sanctuary can take vehicle safaris to learn about the lions' habitats and their role in the web of life we share. If one element of the web goes missing, then everything else can be thrown out of balance. These efforts help everyone understand the importance of living peacefully with all animals, including lions.

Prompt your students with, "Sometimes when we write, we include information that doesn't really belong in that place. This can be confusing for our readers. Let's take a look and see if some information in this paragraph may not belong here."

 **Revision Strategy**

Delete unnecessary information.

Modeling

Display **3.3 Unnecessary Sentence: Part I**, which includes each sentence from the mentor excerpt (as well as an unnecessary sentence that needs to be deleted) numbered in order. For students who could benefit from physically manipulating them, you may choose to display the individual sentences on index cards or sentence strips—or even electronically.

To spark some thinking around deleting unnecessary information, ask students, "What is this paragraph mostly about? How does it answer the question, How can humans and animals both thrive, living near each other and competing for the same resources?" Then share with your students that one sentence in this paragraph does not support the answer to this question. "Something is off in this paragraph. Let's check each sentence, one by one, to see if it ties back to the big idea of this paragraph as it answers the question." Think aloud while modeling how to reread, taking out a different sentence each time, and talk the change through to examine its effect on meaning.

Students talk it out for each sentence using the following questions to prompt the conversation:

- How would deleting this sentence affect the meaning? WHY?
- Do we need this sentence? WHY or WHY NOT?

Through discussion, students determine that sentence #3 doesn't belong because it adds information about the web of life, but doesn't connect to the other sentences that answer the question. It could possibly go somewhere else in the book, but not here. Reveal the original excerpt from *The Lion Queens of India* using the display **3.3 Unnecessary Sentence: Part II**, and compare how the different version affects meaning.

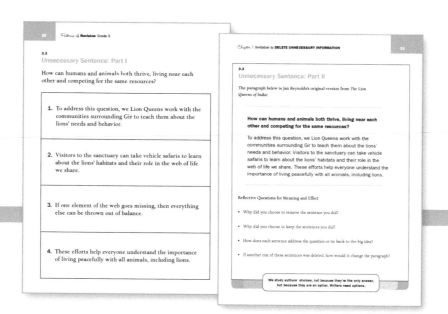

Collaborating Through Conversation

Display **3.3 Invitation to Delete: Part I.** Following the directions provided, students collaborate through conversation to delete the unnecessary sentence. To help students talk it out, remind them to explore how each sentence should support the answer to the question. By justifying their thinking, students take ownership of their decision to delete.

When ready, students compare their deletion choice with others in class, talking through their decisions together. The point here is for them to discuss WHY they made the choice. Display **3.3 Invitation to Delete: Part II** to share the author's original text for comparative analysis, using the reflective questions provided to facilitate a conversation about meaning and effect.

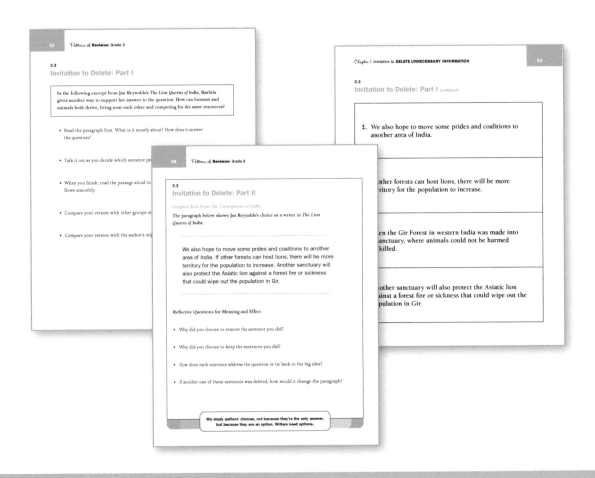

Applying Revision

Students return to their own writing or their writer's notebook and play with deleting unnecessary information and noticing the effect of the removal. If students are practicing how to address a question by writing to a prompt, invite them to check each sentence in their entire piece to ensure that each one supports their answer. Or, if working on another piece that's not prompt driven, students may choose one section or paragraph to revise at a time. It often helps to talk things out with a partner when revising a piece of writing, so invite your writers to self-select into learning pairs if they think it would be helpful (Figure 3.3).

Figure 3.3

Third-grade writers talk out their choices as they revise their own writing.

Sharing Results

Share and celebrate the revision writers did in this lesson. They may have chosen to delete a few words or phrases while others deleted entire sentences, or even paragraphs. Choose one or two students to share their revised selections with the class, naming how the writer effectively used the revision strategy: delete unnecessary information.

3.3

Unnecessary Sentence: Part I

How can humans and animals both thrive, living near each other and competing for the same resources?

1. To address this question, we Lion Queens work with the communities surrounding Gir to teach them about the lions' needs and behavior.

2. Visitors to the sanctuary can take vehicle safaris to learn about the lions' habitats and their role in the web of life we share.

3. If one element of the web goes missing, then everything else can be thrown out of balance.

4. These efforts help everyone understand the importance of living peacefully with all animals, including lions.

3.3

Unnecessary Sentence: Part II

The paragraph below is Jan Reynolds's original version from *The Lion Queens of India:*

How can humans and animals both thrive, living near each other and competing for the same resources?

To address this question, we Lion Queens work with the communities surrounding Gir to teach them about the lions' needs and behavior. Visitors to the sanctuary can take vehicle safaris to learn about the lions' habitats and their role in the web of life we share. These efforts help everyone understand the importance of living peacefully with all animals, including lions.

Reflective Questions for Meaning and Effect

- Why did you choose to remove the sentence you did?

- Why did you choose to keep the sentences you did?

- How does each sentence address the question or tie back to the big idea?

- If another one of these sentences was deleted, how would it change the paragraph?

We study authors' choices, not because they're the only answer, but because they are an option. Writers need options.

3.3

Invitation to Delete: Part I

> In the following excerpt from Jan Reynolds's *The Lion Queens of India*, Rashila gives another way to support her answer to the question: How can humans and animals both thrive, living near each other and competing for the same resources?

- Read the paragraph first. What is it mostly about? How does it answer the question?

- Talk it out as you decide which sentence provides unnecessary information.

- When you finish, read the passage aloud to your group to see if it now flows smoothly.

- Compare your version with other groups or pairs in your class.

- Compare your version with the author's original text.

3.3

Invitation to Delete: Part I *(continued)*

---

1. We also hope to move some prides and coalitions to another area of India.

2. If other forests can host lions, there will be more territory for the population to increase.

3. Then the Gir Forest in western India was made into a sanctuary, where animals could not be harmed or killed.

4. Another sanctuary will also protect the Asiatic lion against a forest fire or sickness that could wipe out the population in Gir.

3.3

Invitation to Delete: Part II

Original Text from *The Lion Queens of India*

The paragraph below shows Jan Reynolds's choice as a writer in *The Lion Queens of India*:

We also hope to move some prides and coalitions to another area of India. If other forests can host lions, there will be more territory for the population to increase. Another sanctuary will also protect the Asiatic lion against a forest fire or sickness that could wipe out the population in Gir.

Reflective Questions for Meaning and Effect

- Why did you choose to remove the sentence you did?

- Why did you choose to keep the sentences you did?

- How does each sentence address the question or tie back to the big idea?

- If another one of these sentences was deleted, how would it change the paragraph?

We study authors' choices, not because they're the only answer, but because they are an option. Writers need options.

Invitation to
REARRANGE

I rearrange a sentence many times. . . . For me, the . . . process feels like a form of play,
like a puzzle that needs solving, and it's one of the most satisfying parts of writing.

– Karen Thompson Walker

Interior designers move furniture and decorations around again and again. They continue adjusting until everything is in just the right place. Writers do this design work as well. We can move words around. We can move phrases around. We can move sentences around. We can even move entire paragraphs around. Meaning and emphasis can change as we rearrange words:

a shower of meteors vs. a meteor shower

Since rearranging can often cause us to make meaning-driven additions and deletions, you'll see your writers calling on strategies they've learned in previous lessons—and dabbling with a few they'll study in future lessons—as they tease out possibilities across this lesson set. Notice how rearranging the preceding example caused us to delete the word *of*, which didn't really change the meaning—but did create a slightly different effect. This is a natural part of rearranging that occurs organically in the discussions you'll have with your writers.

We can move phrases and clauses, too, listening for the most effective options.

When I was little, I ate SpaghettiOs. vs. I ate SpaghettiOs when I was little.

Rearranging opens new possibilities and encourages revisers to play and experiment. Orally talking out arrangement choices and shuffling sequences can bring order out of chaos. Keep it light, keep it playful, and emphasize rearranging is about stretching. If you aren't trying out things and discovering they don't work, you're likely not playing with the words or the order enough.

All the lessons in this chapter follow the same format. We share a paragraph with sentences arranged in an illogical or mixed-up order and then ask students to rearrange them in a way that makes sense. First, we try it out together, then writers try out a different paragraph in small groups or with partners. We conclude each lesson by inviting students to go back to their own writing to consider how they have arranged their ideas and revise in places in which doing so would make their piece more effective. Even if they choose not to keep their original text, we still encourage them to try out a few versions, because we count it as a win any time we can get students revising multiple times, testing out and stretching with possibilities.

The **Rearrange chart** on page 56 can be used as a reference throughout the lessons and beyond. Students may keep a copy in their writing folder, glue a copy into their writing notebook, or access a copy hanging in your classroom.

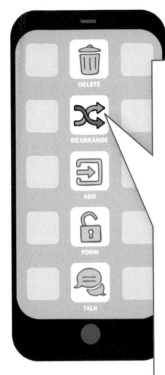

 **REARRANGE**

Rearranging at the **Sentence** Level

Rearranging Words in a Sentence

The cat played with the ball of yarn gently.	to	The cat gently played with the ball of yarn.
Also, Travis plays basketball.	to	Travis also plays basketball.

Rearranging Phrases in a Sentence

Writers can take a phrase and move it to the beginning, in the middle, or at the end of the sentence. You might have to rearrange, add, or delete words or punctuation when you do this.

Phrases that show when	In the meantime, Jeff read a book. Jeff read a book in the meantime.
Phrases that show where	The parade lasted forever on the TV. The parade on the TV lasted forever.
Phrases that show action	Whitney was walking the dogs and saw a cat. While walking the dogs, Whitney saw a cat.

Rearranging Parts of Compound or Complex Sentences

Rearranging a compound sentence	At recess, I went down the slide, and I played with my friends. I played with my friends, and I went down the slide at recess.
Rearranging a complex sentence	While Summer played basketball at recess, Josie twirled on the monkey bars. Josie twirled on the monkey bars while Summer played basketball at recess.

Rearranging at the **Paragraph** Level

Writers can also look at each of the sentences in a paragraph to ensure they are ordered in a way that makes the most sense. Not sure if your sentences are in the best order? Try one of these ideas out:

Break it up!	Break the sentences in your paragraph apart and look at each one separately. Ask yourself if putting them in another order makes sense. If your original order makes the most sense to you, ask yourself why that is. Imagine you had to defend this order of sentences to a classmate or your teacher. What would you say? Talk yourself through why this order makes the most sense. If you notice moving one or more sentences around sounds better, you have the power to do it!
Find a friend	Get a friend or classmate to look at the sentences in one of your paragraphs separated out into individual sentences. Have them put the sentences back together in the order that makes sense to them. Then, have a discussion about why they chose the order they did. If their order is different from your original, you can either talk to your friend/classmate about why you chose a different order, or you can rearrange your sentences to this new order.

3.4 **Rearranger in Time**

Lesson Overview

Revision goal connected to standards:

Develop and strengthen writing by rearranging ideas to ensure a logical progression.

Model Text

Ranger in Time: Disaster on the Titanic
— Written by Kate Messner

Teacher Considerations

A major goal for our young writers is to compose pieces that are clear and tightly connected: ordering ideas, sentences, and paragraphs in a logical way. In this lesson, we focus on this coherence as we invite writers to consider places in their writing that may seem disconnected or illogical. Share the **Rearrange chart** on page 56 with your students. You may decide to have them glue it into their notebook for future reference.

Because books in a series are generally popular among young readers, we chose one of Kate Messner's books from her Ranger in Time series to use with third graders in this lesson. We also love this series because it introduces young readers to historical fiction. Using *Disaster on the Titanic* for this lesson provides a great introduction to the series and will likely get students excited about reading it on their own.

Setting the Context

Before working with the selection we showcase from Chapter 1, get things started by reading the excerpt from the back cover of Kate Messner's *Ranger in Time: Disaster on the Titanic*:

Everyone says the *Titanic* is unsinkable, and Patrick Murphy believes this most of all. He works at the shipyard where the magnificent ship was built, and is even going on its maiden voyage! Ranger meets Patrick before the *Titanic* sets sail, and, once on board, they befriend Maryam and Hamad. But one night, the ship hits an iceberg and starts to take on water. It's a race against time for Ranger and his friends to help get as many passengers—and themselves—off the ship before it's too late!

 **Revision Strategy**

Rearrange and order ideas logically for coherence.

Modeling

Lift the sentences from **3.4 Modeled Sentence Shuffle: Part I** and display them (e.g., on sentence strips or index cards or electronically) face up in no particular order for all students to see. Invite students to begin thinking about the order of the sentences. "These sentences make up the first three sentences of Chapter 1, but they are out of the order Kate chose." We like to use the author's first name when talking with students to show that we are all writers, and this author is one of us. Think aloud as you model ordering the sentences in three different ways, stopping to discuss each order: "Does this make sense? Why or why not? How are things more or less effective this way?"

Once the students feel like they have a logical order in place, display **3.4 Modeled Sentence Shuffle: Part II** to reveal the author's original version and discuss WHY they chose this order. You may choose to use the reflective questions as a guide:

- Why do you think Kate put the sentences in this order?
- Is there another order that would be effective?
- Why do you think our order was different from or the same as Kate's?
- Why might _____ sentence make sense next to/before/after _____ sentence?

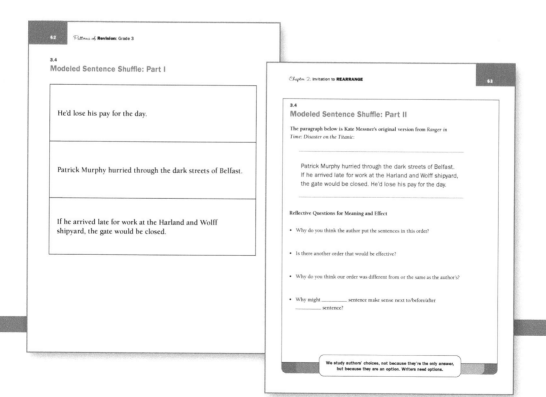

Collaborating Through Conversation

Organize students into pairs or small groups and display the sentences lifted from **3.4 Invitation to Rearrange: Part I**. Following the directions, students collaborate through conversation to order the sentences in a way that seems most logical and effective, discussing why that option seems best or why its ordering wouldn't work.

When ready, students compare their final order with others in class and share their thought processes. Afterward, share the author's original text from **3.4 Invitation to Rearrange: Part II** for comparative analysis. Use the reflective questions at the bottom of the display to facilitate a conversation about meaning and effect as needed.

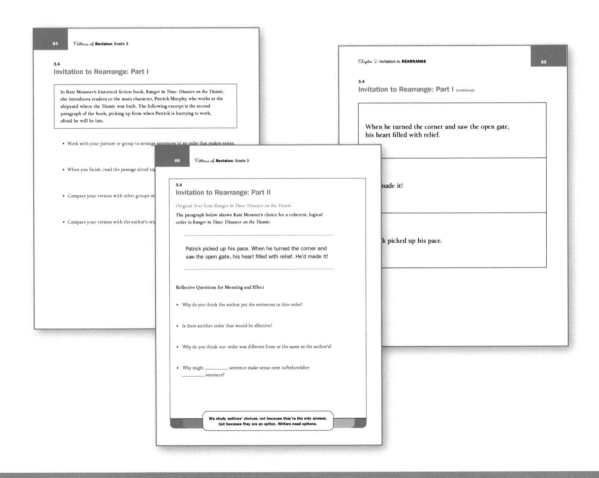

Applying Revision

Students return to their own drafts or writer's notebook and choose one paragraph or a group of sentences to play with revising for order. We suggest giving students strips of paper or sentence strips for them to record each sentence on, so they can physically manipulate the order. (See Figure 3.4.) If writers decide on a more logical order, they can rewrite the sentences on an index card or large sticky note and tape it to their draft. If working on a draft digitally, they can simply cut and paste to rearrange things to their liking. If time permits, have them repeat this process with another section of their draft or take a look at the draft as a whole, ensuring a logical progression, and revising for order as needed.

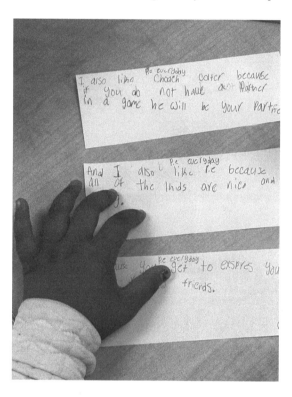

Figure 3.4

This third-grade writer chose to write some of her sentences on strips to consider the most effective order of them.

Sharing Results

To celebrate their revisions, invite writers to share with someone in the class. Allow time for them to discuss their reordered sentences with a classmate or small group, noting as they do the effects of the reordering and evaluating each version for meaning and effect. Take pictures or ask to keep a few examples as models of revision for future lessons, this year and beyond.

3.4
Modeled Sentence Shuffle: Part I

He'd lose his pay for the day.

Patrick Murphy hurried through the dark streets of Belfast.

If he arrived late for work at the Harland and Wolff shipyard, the gate would be closed.

3.4

Modeled Sentence Shuffle: Part II

The paragraph below is Kate Messner's original version from *Ranger in Time: Disaster on the Titanic*:

Patrick Murphy hurried through the dark streets of Belfast. If he arrived late for work at the Harland and Wolff shipyard, the gate would be closed. He'd lose his pay for the day.

Reflective Questions for Meaning and Effect

- Why do you think the author put the sentences in this order?

- Is there another order that would be effective?

- Why do you think our order was different from or the same as the author's?

- Why might _____ sentence make sense next to/before/after _____ sentence?

> **We study authors' choices, not because they're the only answer, but because they are an option. Writers need options.**

3.4

Invitation to Rearrange: Part I

In Kate Messner's historical fiction book, *Ranger in Time: Disaster on the Titanic*, she introduces readers to the main character, Patrick Murphy, who works at the shipyard where the *Titanic* was built. The following excerpt is the second paragraph of the book, picking up from when Patrick is hurrying to work, afraid he will be late.

- Work with your partner or group to arrange sentences in an order that makes sense.

- When you finish, read the passage aloud together to see if the order works.

- Compare your version with other groups or pairs in your class.

- Compare your version with the author's original text.

3.4

Invitation to Rearrange: Part I *(continued)*

When he turned the corner and saw the open gate,
his heart filled with relief.

He'd made it!

Patrick picked up his pace.

3.4

Invitation to Rearrange: Part II

Original Text from *Ranger in Time: Disaster on the Titanic*

The paragraph below shows Kate Messner's choice for a coherent, logical order in *Ranger in Time: Disaster on the Titanic*:

Patrick picked up his pace. When he turned the corner and saw the open gate, his heart filled with relief. He'd made it!

Reflective Questions for Meaning and Effect

- Why do you think the author put the sentences in this order?

- Is there another order that would be effective?

- Why do you think our order was different from or the same as the author's?

- Why might _____ sentence make sense next to/before/after _____ sentence?

We study authors' choices, not because they're the only answer, but because they are an option. Writers need options.

3.5 **Sorting Sentences**

Lesson Overview

Revision goal connected to standards:

Develop and strengthen writing by rearranging ideas to ensure a logical progression.

Model Text

Billy Miller Makes a Wish
  – Written by Kevin Henkes

Teacher Considerations

In this lesson we continue to focus on coherence as we invite writers to consider places in their writing that may seem disconnected or illogical, while adding the use of time-order words to help with sequencing. Kevin Henkes chooses to use time-order words like *first, then*, and *soon* at the beginning of some sentences and at the end of others. We like using this model to show students that sequential words don't always have to come at the beginning of a sentence, nor does every sentence need one. As readers, we visualize. As writers, we want to provide information in an order that helps our readers visualize how things unfold. This lesson provides opportunities for our students to do this work as both readers and writers.

This lesson begins with the oral reading of an excerpt. We then take part of that excerpt and present it out of order, and we invite students to organize it in ways that makes sense through conversations about meaning and effect. We especially encourage them to take time to visualize the text and discuss why each sentence needs to go where it does as we consider mental images and chronological order.

Setting the Context

Billy Miller Makes a Wish, a companion to Newbery Honor *The Year of Billy Miller*, is a book about a boy who turns eight and makes a wish for something exciting to happen when he blows out his birthday candles. Readers are then taken through a summer of excitement in Billy's life before third grade.

To set a context, explain that in Chapter 10 of Kevin Henkes's *Billy Miller Makes a Wish*, Billy and his younger sister, Sal, are trying to help their mom organize the basement. Billy decides to give Sal a job of sorting letters like a mail carrier to keep her busy.

Then read aloud the following excerpt:

Billy found the box of letters and dragged it over to Sal. Quickly, she got to work. She sank to her knees and began making piles. First she separated the letters by size. Then she placed all the colored envelopes together. She picked out the envelopes with postage stamps she particularly liked and put them in the buggy first.

She talked as she sorted, her soft, clear voice rising and falling as if she were chirping a song. Billy couldn't make out what she was saying, but she was busy—that was what mattered.

Revision Strategy

Rearrange and order ideas logically for coherence.

Modeling

Lift the sentences from **3.5 Modeled Sentence Shuffle: Part I** and display them (e.g., on sentence strips or index cards or electronically) face up in no particular order for all students to see. Invite students to consider the order of the sentences. "These sentences from part of the read-aloud are out of order." Think aloud as you model ordering the sentences in three different ways, stopping to discuss each order: "Does this make sense? Why or why not? How are things more or less effective this way?"

When the students feel like the order they chose is logically in place, revisit Kevin Henkes's original version on the display page **3.5 Modeled Sentence Shuffle: Part I**, comparing his order to that of the class, and discussing WHY he likely chose this order. In this excerpt, the time-order words help to establish a logical order, so encourage your students to think about the word choice Henkes used as they interact.

You may choose to use the reflective questions as a guide:

- Why do you think Kevin put the sentences in this order?
- Is there another order that would be effective?
- Why do you think our order was different from or the same as Kevin's?
- What words helped you think about the order?

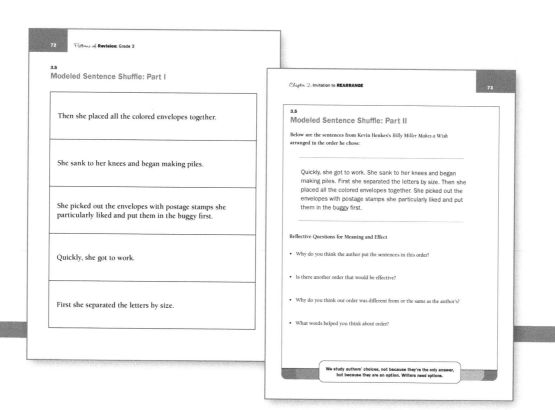

Collaborating Through Conversation

Display the sentences lifted from **3.5 Invitation to Rearrange: Part I** (e.g., on index cards or sentence strips or electronically). Following the directions, students collaborate through conversation to order the sentences in a way that makes sense and helps the reader visualize the order of events.

When ready, students compare their order with others in class, sharing their thought processes. Afterward, use the display page **3.5 Invitation to Rearrange: Part II** to share Kevin Henkes's original text for comparative analysis. Use the reflective questions provided to facilitate a conversation about meaning and effect.

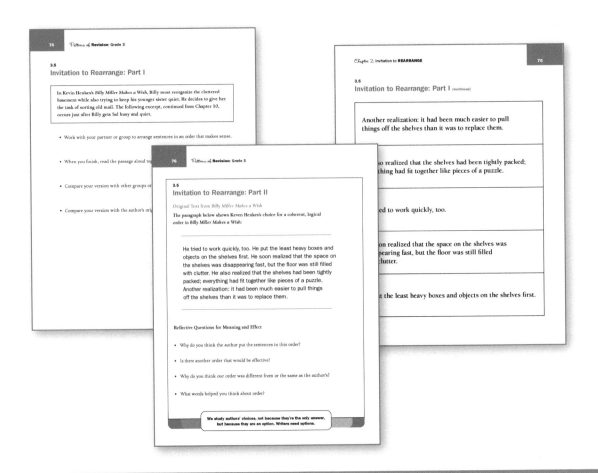

Applying Revision

Students return to current or past drafts or their writer's notebook and play with order, noticing effect and rearranging as needed. They may choose to focus on one section or paragraph at a time. (See Figure 3.5.) Some writers may find that an entire paragraph needs to go to another place in the piece. It's all about meaning and effect. What makes the most sense?

In this process, writers have options. They may choose to write the sentences from their chosen section on strips to rearrange. They may also decide to look at the piece as whole, making sure it flows smoothly, asking a partner to help them. For narrative writing, invite students act out a scene, checking to make sure they've included each detail in a logical order, or invite them to make a quick sketch to illustrate how they want their readers to imagine that part, like a page from a graphic novel. Then, have them go back in their draft to see if that selection shows the order in a way that's clear for their readers. Do any time-order words need to be added to help the reader visualize?

Figure 3.5

This writer uses a sticky note to help rearrange some of his ideas.

Sharing Results

Students pair up to share their revisions from the lesson. Allow time for them to discuss why they chose to order their sentences in a particular way, and what words they used to help guide their readers. Celebrate these revisions with feedback that names how the students used the revision strategy: Rearrange and order ideas logically for coherence.

3.5

Modeled Sentence Shuffle: Part I

Then she placed all the colored envelopes together.

She sank to her knees and began making piles.

She picked out the envelopes with postage stamps she particularly liked and put them in the buggy first.

Quickly, she got to work.

First she separated the letters by size.

3.5

Modeled Sentence Shuffle: Part II

Below are the sentences from Kevin Henkes's *Billy Miller Makes a Wish* arranged in the order he chose:

Quickly, she got to work. She sank to her knees and began making piles. First she separated the letters by size. Then she placed all the colored envelopes together. She picked out the envelopes with postage stamps she particularly liked and put them in the buggy first.

Reflective Questions for Meaning and Effect

- Why do you think the author put the sentences in this order?

- Is there another order that would be effective?

- Why do you think our order was different from or the same as the author's?

- What words helped you think about order?

We study authors' choices, not because they're the only answer, but because they are an option. Writers need options.

3.5

Invitation to Rearrange: Part I

In Kevin Henkes's *Billy Miller Makes a Wish,* Billy must reorganize the cluttered basement while also trying to keep his younger sister quiet. He decides to give her the task of sorting old mail. The following excerpt, continued from Chapter 10, occurs just after Billy gets Sal busy and quiet.

- Work with your partner or group to arrange sentences in an order that makes sense.

- When you finish, read the passage aloud together to see if order works.

- Compare your version with other groups or pairs in your class.

- Compare your version with the author's original text.

3.5

Invitation to Rearrange: Part I *(continued)*

Another realization: it had been much easier to pull things off the shelves than it was to replace them.

He also realized that the shelves had been tightly packed; everything had fit together like pieces of a puzzle.

He tried to work quickly, too.

He soon realized that the space on the shelves was disappearing fast, but the floor was still filled with clutter.

He put the least heavy boxes and objects on the shelves first.

3.5

Invitation to Rearrange: Part II

Original Text from *Billy Miller Makes a Wish*

The paragraph below shows Keven Henkes's choice for a coherent, logical order in *Billy Miller Makes a Wish*:

He tried to work quickly, too. He put the least heavy boxes and objects on the shelves first. He soon realized that the space on the shelves was disappearing fast, but the floor was still filled with clutter. He also realized that the shelves had been tightly packed; everything had fit together like pieces of a puzzle. Another realization: it had been much easier to pull things off the shelves than it was to replace them.

Reflective Questions for Meaning and Effect

- Why do you think the author put the sentences in this order?

- Is there another order that would be effective?

- Why do you think our order was different from or the same as the author's?

- What words helped you think about order?

We study authors' choices, not because they're the only answer, but because they are an option. Writers need options.

3.6 Take Action and Rearrange

Lesson Overview

Revision goal connected to standards:

Develop and strengthen writing by rearranging ideas to ensure a logical progression.

Model Text

Stand Up! 10 Mighty Women Who Made a Change
- Written by Brittney Cooper
- Illustrated by Cathy Ann Johnson

Teacher Considerations

Now that students have spent some time revising for order with narrative texts, we move into this lesson to explore how nonfiction authors are careful to arrange their writing in a logical way as well. In *Stand Up! 10 Mighty Women Who Made a Change*, Brittney Cooper uses a variety of text structures and points of view to celebrate Black women who have taken a stand against injustice. This lesson invites students into conversations about how Brittney uses main ideas with details to organize the sentences in her paragraphs. We chose to use the selection about Mari Copeny as our mentor, breaking it into two parts: one for the modeling and the other for collaboration through conversation. We suggest studying the selection together in its entirety afterward, to look beyond the sentence level and consider how paragraphs are also arranged to connect ideas in a logical progression.

Setting the Context

To set a context, read aloud the following excerpt to introduce your students to Mari Copeny, one of the women showcased in Brittney Cooper's *Stand Up! 10 Mighty Women Who Made a Change* with the following excerpt:

Mari Copeny is from the town of Flint, Michigan.

Every child in her neighborhood learned not to drink the water from the faucet. It was deadly. An accident had poisoned Flint's water, but nobody did anything to clean it. Nobody in the government seemed to care. Mari Copeny thought clean water was a basic human right, so she decided to do something about it.

 **Revision Strategy**

Rearrange and order ideas logically for coherence.

Modeling

Lift the sentences from **3.6 Modeled Sentence Shuffle: Part I**, and display them (e.g., on sentence strips or index cards or electronically) face up in no particular order for all students to see. Invite students to consider how the ideas are connected and talk about how they might be logically ordered. "These are some of the sentences from the excerpt I just read aloud, but they are out of order." Think aloud as you model ordering the sentences in different ways, stopping to discuss each order: "Does this make sense? Why or why not? What would happen if I put this sentence before this one?"

Once the class feels like the ideas are connected logically, reveal Brittney Cooper's original version and compare the class's order to Brittney's, discussing the effect of each, using the display page **3.6 Modeled Sentence Shuffle: Part II**.

You may choose to use the reflective questions as a guide:

- Why do you think the Brittney put the sentences in this order?
- Is there another order that would be effective?
- Why do you think our order was different from or the same as Brittney's?
- Why might _____ sentence make sense next to/before/after _____ sentence?

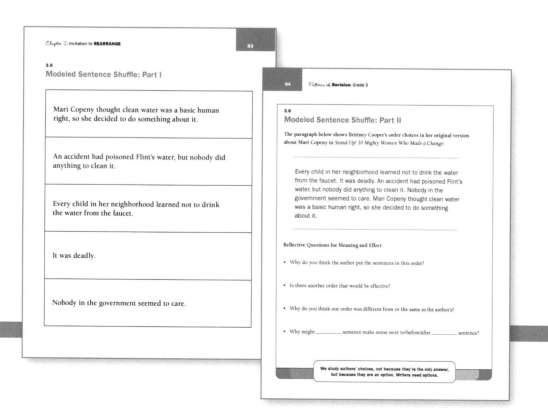

3.6
Modeled Sentence Shuffle: Part I

Mari Copeny thought clean water was a basic human right, so she decided to do something about it.

An accident had poisoned Flint's water, but nobody did anything to clean it.

Every child in her neighborhood learned not to drink the water from the faucet.

It was deadly.

Nobody in the government seemed to care.

84   *Patterns of* **Revision**: Grade 3

3.6
Modeled Sentence Shuffle: Part II

The paragraph below shows Brittney Cooper's order choices in her original version about Mari Copeny in *Stand Up! 10 Mighty Women Who Made a Change:*

Every child in her neighborhood learned not to drink the water from the faucet. It was deadly. An accident had poisoned Flint's water, but nobody did anything to clean it. Nobody in the government seemed to care. Mari Copeny thought clean water was a basic human right, so she decided to do something about it.

Reflective Questions for Meaning and Effect

- Why do you think the author put the sentences in this order?

- Is there another order that would be effective?

- Why do you think our order was different from or the same as the author's?

- Why might _____ sentence make sense next to/before/after _____ sentence?

We study authors' choices, not because they're the only answer, but because they are an option. Writers need options.

Collaborating Through Conversation

Display the sentences lifted from **3.6 Invitation to Rearrange: Part I** (e.g., on index cards or sentence strips or electronically). In pairs or small groups, students collaborate through conversation to order the sentences in a way that makes sense and tightly connects the ideas.

When ready, students compare their order with others in class and share why they chose the order they did. Afterward, using **3.6 Invitation to Rearrange: Part II**, display Brittney Cooper's original text for comparative analysis. Use the reflective questions provided to facilitate a conversation about meaning and effect.

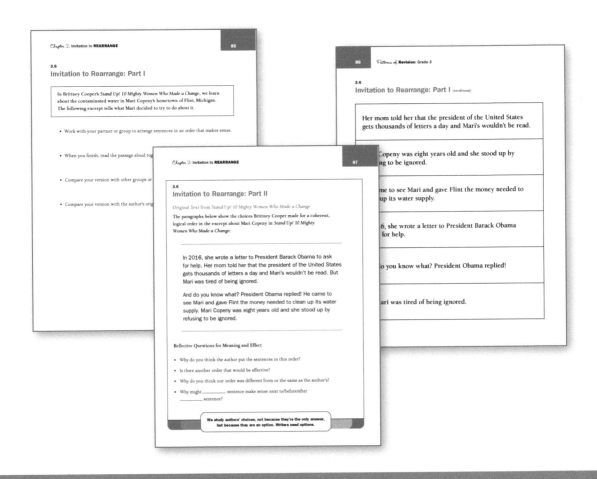

Applying Revision

Students return to their own draft or writer's notebook and play with order, noticing its effect and rearranging as needed. This revision strategy can be used at any part of the writing process, so remind students that their draft does not need to be complete before rearranging. Many times, rearranging comes within the planning stage of the writing process as well. Students may choose to focus on one section or paragraph at a time. Some students may find that an entire paragraph needs to go to another place in the piece. It may be helpful for students to cut up their piece with scissors, either by sentence or by paragraph, and physically rearrange their piece. Then, they can glue or tape the new order onto a piece of construction paper. As they work, students may also discover a part that needs to be deleted. Remind writers of the other revision strategies they have learned, and invite them to apply those as well. It's all about meaning and effect. What makes the most sense?

Sharing Results

To celebrate the revision writers did in this lesson, students share results with partners. Allow time to discuss revisions, noting the effect of the reordered sentences and providing feedback to each other about how the ideas are connected. Invite students to write a piece of feedback on a sticky note and place it on top of their partner's piece:

I noticed that you _____. This helps me as a reader because _____.

Extending the Conversation

As an extension to this lesson, you may also choose to use the entire selection about Mari Copeny as mentor for your students to use during application. Since third graders are likely writing essays with paragraphs, it is often helpful to see a mentor text written in this format. We've provided it as an additional printable at the end of this lesson for your students to have in front of them while considering how to group ideas into paragraphs as they play around with order and revision at the whole text level.

Invite your students to share their thinking about the order of the paragraphs within the piece using the following guiding questions:

- What makes this order effective?
- What would happen if we moved this paragraph to the top?
- (Point to the beginning of one of the paragraphs.) Why do you think the author chose to begin a new paragraph here? What would happen if it were combined with the previous paragraph?
- Let's look at the very first sentence of the piece. How does the author use the sentence to set up the rest of the text?
- What about the closing sentence? What would happen if the closing sentence was moved somewhere else?

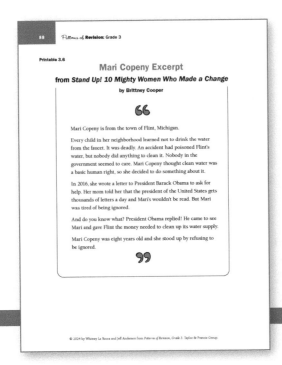

3.6

Modeled Sentence Shuffle: Part I

Mari Copeny thought clean water was a basic human right, so she decided to do something about it.

An accident had poisoned Flint's water, but nobody did anything to clean it.

Every child in her neighborhood learned not to drink the water from the faucet.

It was deadly.

Nobody in the government seemed to care.

3.6

Modeled Sentence Shuffle: Part II

The paragraph below shows Brittney Cooper's order choices in her original version about Mari Copeny in *Stand Up! 10 Mighty Women Who Made a Change*:

Every child in her neighborhood learned not to drink the water from the faucet. It was deadly. An accident had poisoned Flint's water, but nobody did anything to clean it. Nobody in the government seemed to care. Mari Copeny thought clean water was a basic human right, so she decided to do something about it.

Reflective Questions for Meaning and Effect

- Why do you think the author put the sentences in this order?

- Is there another order that would be effective?

- Why do you think our order was different from or the same as the author's?

- Why might _____ sentence make sense next to/before/after _____ sentence?

> **We study authors' choices, not because they're the only answer, but because they are an option. Writers need options.**

3.6

Invitation to Rearrange: Part I

> In Brittney Cooper's *Stand Up! 10 Mighty Women Who Made a Change*, we learn about the contaminated water in Mari Copeny's hometown of Flint, Michigan. The following excerpt tells what Mari decided to try to do about it.

- Work with your partner or group to arrange sentences in an order that makes sense.

- When you finish, read the passage aloud together to see if order works.

- Compare your version with other groups or pairs in your class.

- Compare your version with the author's original text.

(continues)

3.6

Invitation to Rearrange: Part I *(continued)*

Her mom told her that the president of the United States gets thousands of letters a day and Mari's wouldn't be read.

Mari Copeny was eight years old and she stood up by refusing to be ignored.

He came to see Mari and gave Flint the money needed to clean up its water supply.

In 2016, she wrote a letter to President Barack Obama to ask for help.

And do you know what? President Obama replied!

But Mari was tired of being ignored.

3.6

Invitation to Rearrange: Part II

Original Text from *Stand Up! 10 Mighty Women Who Made a Change*

The paragraphs below show the choices Brittney Cooper made for a coherent, logical order in the excerpt about Mari Copeny in *Stand Up! 10 Mighty Women Who Made a Change*:

In 2016, she wrote a letter to President Barack Obama to ask for help. Her mom told her that the president of the United States gets thousands of letters a day and Mari's wouldn't be read. But Mari was tired of being ignored.

And do you know what? President Obama replied! He came to see Mari and gave Flint the money needed to clean up its water supply. Mari Copeny was eight years old and she stood up by refusing to be ignored.

Reflective Questions for Meaning and Effect

- Why do you think the author put the sentences in this order?

- Is there another order that would be effective?

- Why do you think our order was different from or the same as the author's?

- Why might _____ sentence make sense next to/before/after _____ sentence?

> We study authors' choices, not because they're the only answer, but because they are an option. Writers need options.

Printable 3.6

Mari Copeny Excerpt

from *Stand Up! 10 Mighty Women Who Made a Change*

by Brittney Cooper

Mari Copeny is from the town of Flint, Michigan.

Every child in her neighborhood learned not to drink the water from the faucet. It was deadly. An accident had poisoned Flint's water, but nobody did anything to clean it. Nobody in the government seemed to care. Mari Copeny thought clean water was a basic human right, so she decided to do something about it.

In 2016, she wrote a letter to President Barack Obama to ask for help. Her mom told her that the president of the United States gets thousands of letters a day and Mari's wouldn't be read. But Mari was tired of being ignored.

And do you know what? President Obama replied! He came to see Mari and gave Flint the money needed to clean up its water supply.

Mari Copeny was eight years old and she stood up by refusing to be ignored.

Invitation to
ADD CONNECTORS

*We are wired for connection. But the key is that, in any given moment of it,
it has to be real.*

– Brené Brown

E. M. Forster wrote, "Only connect." We round out the lesson sets in Part I with adding connectors because—as you move into Part II—you'll find that connectors are the glue that hold our writing together, shifting from one idea to the next, helping our readers move through the text. When a writer is combining sentences, connectors are a fabulous friend. Consider how these connectors help transition or link ideas and help define the relationship between and among ideas:

- *And*
- *Or*
- *But*
- *So*
- *Although*
- *When*
- *While*

Connectors may also include phrases that writers add in to join ideas and make their message clearer:

- *In other words,*
- *For example,*
- *When* _____*,*
- *Like* _____*,*
- *If* _____*,*

Third graders often have a flurry of ideas, drafting sentence after sentence to get it all on the page before they forget. If you see that writers include too many short, choppy sentences or are struggling with repetition in their writing, a need for more connectors may be the culprit. You'll immediately notice an elevation in your third graders' writing as they learn to add in connectors, such as transitional words, conjunctions, or sentences, to help connect their ideas, making their message more coherent for the reader. Building this awareness that writers use connectors to link their ideas is crucial to the development of third-grade writing and reading. As writers, they begin to see the options and effects in discussions. As readers they become more likely to notice shifts in ideas, aiding in comprehension.

Tip

Connectors aren't limited just to words and phrases. Punctuation marks are essential connectors as well. And, although all punctuation separates, notice how these punctuation marks also connect or join ideas or sentences:

- Commas
- Colon
- Dash
- Semicolon

The reciprocal nature of reading, writing, and grammar are not lost during revision.

Connectors are primarily thought of as punctuation marks or words, especially conjunctions and relative pronouns. (For more information on connector words and punctuation, please refer to **The Connectors chart** located on page 92. This chart is another student page from *Patterns of Revision* that can be kept in writer's notebooks, binders, folders—digital or analog.) To support the concept of adding connectors for third-grade revisers in this chapter of lessons, we select a sentence that connects ideas sequentially or clarifies information while maintaining focus. Just like connector words, writers explore how adding transitional sentences can serve the purpose of sequence. The **Add chart** on page 91 can be used as a reference throughout the lessons and beyond. Students may keep a copy in their writing folder, glue a copy into their writing notebook, or access a copy hanging in your classroom. As always, we try the process out together first, then writers try out a different example in small groups or with partners. We conclude the lesson by inviting students to return to their own writing to add connecting ideas, whether with sentences, phrases, or words that might help clarify the writer's message or purpose.

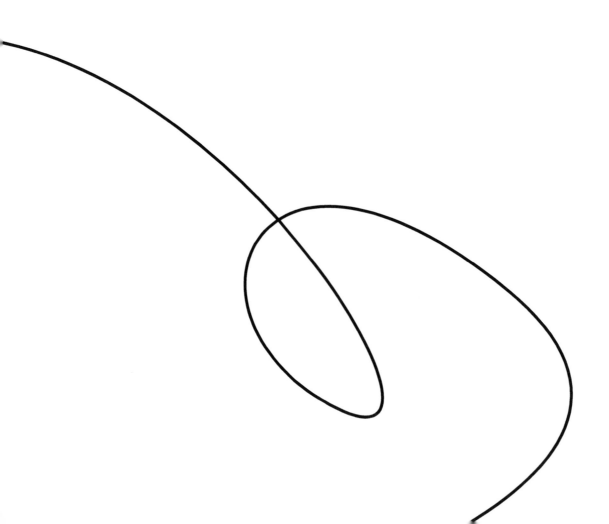

Adding Connectors at the Sentence Level	
Prepositions	Adding a preposition (or a prepositional phrase) grounds the reader in time and place. They can also introduce examples, contrasts, or comparisons. *Without a glass of milk, cookies aren't as delicious.*
Conjunctions	Subordinating conjunctions show relationships between ideas, sometimes making one idea more or less important than another. They are used within complex sentences. *When I bake cookies, a delicious aroma fills the air.* Coordinating conjunctions make connections that are equal to each other. They can join sentences to create compound sentences, and they can also show a relationship between a pair or a list. *I like to bake cookies, but I will only eat them with a glass of milk.*
Relative Pronouns	Introduces or links additional information to the noun before it. *Cookies that have large chocolate chunks in them are better than plain chocolate chip cookies.*
Punctuation	Combines, introduces, and encloses information within a sentence. *Cookies, for example, are best when dipped in milk.*

Adding Connectors at the Paragraph Level

Add a sentence (or even a paragraph or more) . . .
- to the beginning of a paragraph to introduce the new main idea, or to transition to a new idea.
- to transition from one idea to the next.
- to add important information to the sentence before.
- to move the reader through time.

The Connectors

Prepositions
What do they do? *They show time and place as well as introduce examples, contrasts, or comparisons.*

Function	Example
Time	*at, in, on*
Extended Time	*by, during, for, from, since, to, until, with(in)*
Direction	*in, into, on, onto, to, toward*
Location	*above, across, against, ahead of, along, among, around, at, behind, below, beneath, beside, between, by, from, in, inside, near, of, off, on, out, over, through, toward, under, within*
Introduce Examples and Comparisons or Contrasts	*as, despite, except, for, like, of, per, than, with, without*

Relative Pronouns
What do they do? *Introduce and link additional information to the noun before it.*

Function	Example
Link **ideas and things** to more detail	*that, what, which*
Link **people** to more detail	*who, whoever, whom, whose*

Subordinating Conjunctions (AAAWWUBBIS)
Although
As
After
While
When
Until
Because
Before
If
Since

What do they do? *They show relationships, sometimes making one idea more or less important.*

Function	Example
Time	*after, before, during, since, until, when, whenever, while*
Cause-Effect	*as, because, since, so*
Opposition	*although, even though, though, whatever, while*
Condition	*as long as, if, in order to, unless, until, whatever*

Coordinating Conjunctions (FANBOYS)
For
And
Nor
But
Or
Yet
So

What do they do? *They make connections that are equal to each other. They join sentences (thereby making compound sentences), and they can show a relationship between a pair or a list.*

Connector Punctuation
What do they do? *They combine, introduce, and enclose information.*

Combines	Introduces	Encloses	Function	Example
Comma ,		Comma ,	Combine	*and*
Dash —	Dash —	Dash —	Opposition	*but, nor, yet*
Semicolon ;	Colon :	Parentheses ( )	Cause-Effect	*for, so*
		Quotation Marks " "	Choice	*or*

3.7 Like Gecko Feet: Clarifying Information Keeps Your Writing Together

Lesson Overview

Revision goal connected to standards:

Develop and strengthen writing by adding information and ideas for coherence and clarity.

Model Text

Mimic Makers: Biomimicry Inventors Inspired by Nature
- – Written by Kristen Nordstrom
- – Illustrated by Paul Boston

Teacher Considerations

Because we learn from other authors as writers, taking what they do in their writing and trying it out, or mimicking it, in our own writing, we thought using Nordstrom's *Mimic Makers* for our first lesson on adding connectors could act as a metaphor for this. Although our model text is nonfiction, the revision strategy we home in on can be used within all genres. Our focus here is on adding a sentence or multiple sentences to clarify for the reader, connecting ideas together. Notice the precise words Nordstrom uses to help clarify information for readers. During the discussion, you may choose to weave her word choice into the conversation. When students set off to do this work on their own, we invite them to determine parts in their writing that leave their reader with questions. Writers can then add clarifying information to help answer those questions. You may choose to hang the **Add chart** (page 91) in your classroom or have your students glue it into their notebooks for reference.

Since this is the first lesson on adding connectors, you may choose to incorporate more guidance during the discussion. If you do, be sure to leave ample time for this, keeping this lesson focused on your students' thoughts and discoveries rather than a checklist of tasks.

Setting the Context

In *Mimic Makers: Biomimicry Inventors Inspired by Nature*, Kristen Nordstrom introduces students to ten inventors who imitated something they studied in nature, such as the leaves of a tree, to create a new technology to help people. To set the context, read aloud the following excerpt from *Mimic Makers* (page 36) about two scientists who were inspired by a tokay gecko.

DUNCAN IRSCHICK and ALFRED CROSBY watched tokay geckos walk up walls and saunter across ceilings. They wanted to know this lizard's sticky tricks. Under a high-powered microscope, they observed that the gecko's toe pads were covered with thousands of tiny bristles, called setae.

Now read aloud the following paragraph. *Shh!* We've removed a sentence from the original paragraph, but don't tell your students that. Reveal the original version later.

Through many experiments, Duncan and Alfred explored how these setae work with the tendons in a gecko's foot. They are flexible, which helps the gecko's foot mold to a surface. They are also stiff, which helps hold the foot firmly in place.

Prompt students with, "Guess what? A sentence has gone missing from this paragraph. Did you notice? When information is missing, the reader may be left with questions, needing more information."

 Revision Strategy
Add a connector, a sentence or sentences, to clarify information for your reader.

Modeling

Display **3.7 Something's Missing: Part I**, which has the mentor excerpt that shows where a new clarifying sentence needs to be inserted. "The writer of this paragraph needs to revise by adding a sentence that clarifies information. Let's a look at this paragraph in which something's missing." Discuss the author's message in the existing parts around the blank. Possible questions to prompt discussion:

- "What is Kristen saying in the first sentence?"
- "What is Kristen's message in the sentences that follow the blank?"
- "What do you notice about the writing before/after the blank space?"

Invite students to consider which of the three starred sentence choices could be added to the author's writing. Model trying out one of the sentences, reading it in the paragraph, and discussing WHY that option works or doesn't work well. Steer the conversation toward meaning and effect rather than right or wrong. Continue to model the other two starred options or invite students to try them and talk them out in pairs or small groups.

Reveal Kristen Nordstrom's original version at the end, using the display page, **3.7 Something's Missing: Part II**, for further discussion and comparative analysis. You may choose to use these reflective questions as a guide:

- Why do you think the author used this sentence?
- Do any of the other starred sentence options work? Why or why not?
- Why do you think your choice was different from or the same as the author's?

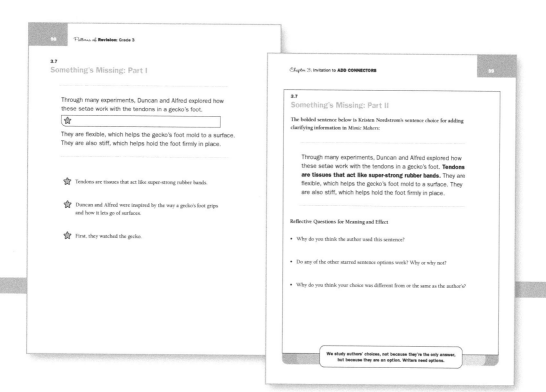

Collaborating Through Conversation

Display **3.7 Invitation to Add Connectors: Part I**. In pairs or small groups, students collaborate through conversation with one or more classmates to select the sentence they think makes the best clarifying add-in. The conversation is key. Talking it out is revision. As students work, help them focus their conversations on meaning and effect—what works, what doesn't, and why—as opposed to which options are right or wrong. When ready, students compare their add-in sentence with others in class, discussing WHY they chose their specific add-in over the other options. Then share Kristen Nordstrom's original text for comparative analysis, using **3.7 Invitation to Add Connectors: Part II**. Use the reflective questions at the bottom of the display to facilitate further conversations about meaning and effect.

Applying Revision

Students return to their own writing or their writer's notebook and use Kristen Nordstrom as their mentor for adding a sentence or phrase that clarifies information. Students choose one part or one paragraph of their writing to focus on. Possible prompts include:

- What are you saying in the first sentence?
- What is your message or main idea in the sentences that follow?
- How do your ideas link together? Is there anything missing?
- What questions might your reader have here? What could you add to help answer these questions?

Students can insert their additional sentences or phrases in their writing using a carat, a sticky note, or a strip of paper taped onto their piece. They may also choose to focus on word choice, making sure they are using precise words that directly connect to their topic. If time allows, students repeat this revision process in another part of their writing or even in another piece (Figure 3.7).

Figure 3.7

A third-grade writer adds clarifying information to their draft using a strip of paper.

> How do dolPhins Swim?
> One Part On how they Swim is they
> move thier taiß uP and down to
> Swim forward, and use thier fiPPers
> to turn, Steer and Stop.
> DolPhins Steer because it helps them turn

Sharing Results

Celebrate the revision writers did in this lesson with a sharing session. Some students may have chosen to add in a few words or phrases, and others might have added in entire sentences. Invite writers to jot why they added information on a sticky note to display next to their writing in preparation for a gallery walk.

3.7
Something's Missing: Part I

Through many experiments, Duncan and Alfred explored how these setae work with the tendons in a gecko's foot.

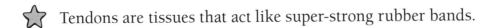

They are flexible, which helps the gecko's foot mold to a surface. They are also stiff, which helps hold the foot firmly in place.

 Tendons are tissues that act like super-strong rubber bands.

 Duncan and Alfred were inspired by the way a gecko's foot grips and how it lets go of surfaces.

 First, they watched the gecko.

3.7
Something's Missing: Part II

The bolded sentence below is Kristen Nordstrom's sentence choice for adding clarifying information in *Mimic Makers*:

Through many experiments, Duncan and Alfred explored how these setae work with the tendons in a gecko's foot. **Tendons are tissues that act like super-strong rubber bands.** They are flexible, which helps the gecko's foot mold to a surface. They are also stiff, which helps hold the foot firmly in place.

Reflective Questions for Meaning and Effect

- Why do you think the author used this sentence?

- Do any of the other starred sentence options work? Why or why not?

- Why do you think your choice was different from or the same as the author's?

We study authors' choices, not because they're the only answer, but because they are an option. Writers need options.

3.7

Invitation to Add Connectors: Part I

> In *Mimic Makers*, Kristen Nordstrom shares how Duncan Irschick and Alfred Crosby studied the tokay gecko and used what they learned to invent Geckskin, a strong sticky pad that works like the feet of geckos. In this excerpt, Kirsten continues to share more information about the process of this invention.

- Read the paragraph on the next page.

- Study what the paragraph is mainly describing.

- Look closely at the first sentence before the blank as well as the ones after the blank.

- Try each starred sentence in the blank and decide which one makes the most sense.

- Compare your version with other groups or pairs.

- Compare and contrast your version with the author's original text.

3.7

Invitation to Add Connectors: Part I *(continued)*

Duncan and Alfred were inspired by the way a gecko's foot grips and lets go of surfaces. First they invented a prototype called Geckskin. Next they invented products based on this working model. These products stick to a surface, hold on tight, and let go when needed.

Maybe one day, as these products develop, you'll be able to use Geckskin to saunter across the ceiling.

 It is made of two parts: a soft nylon that sticks like tape to a surface and a stiff woven fabric that holds the connection in place.

 You can really get a grip with Geckskin technology.

 You can use them to hang all sorts of things: pictures, lights, and even tools.

3.7

Invitation to Add Connectors: Part II

Original Text from *Mimic Makers: Biomimicry Inventors Inspired by Nature*

The bolded sentence below is Kristen Nordstrom's sentence choice for adding clarifying information in *Mimic Makers*:

Duncan and Alfred were inspired by the way a gecko's foot grips and lets go of surfaces. First they invented a prototype called Geckskin. Next they invented products based on this working model. These products stick to a surface, hold on tight, and let go when needed. **You can use them to hang all sorts of things: pictures, lights, and even tools.** Maybe one day, as these products develop, you'll be able to use Geckskin to saunter across the ceiling.

Reflective Questions for Meaning and Effect

- Why do you think the author used this sentence?

- Do any of the other starred sentence options work? Why or why not?

- Why do you think your choice was different from or the same as the author's?

> **We study authors' choices, not because they're the only answer, but because they are an option. Writers need options.**

3.8 Take the Liberty to Add Connecting Sentences

Lesson Overview

Revision goal connected to standards:

Develop and strengthen writing by adding sentences to connect ideas, giving the paragraph or piece coherence.

Model Text

Let Liberty Rise! How America's Schoolchildren Helped Save the Statue of Liberty
- Written by Chana Stiefel
- Illustrated by Chuck Groenink

Teacher Considerations

When revising, writers check for coherence: making sure each idea connects to the next. We use this lesson to home in on this even more, thinking about how our ideas are related and making sure our paragraphs, as well as the entire piece, are coherent. Sometimes, we'll add a sentence that includes a transition word to connect the ideas, and other times, the sentences we insert will add information to connect our ideas. (See **The Connectors chart** on page 92.) This lesson is a chance to play with connections at this broader level. The next lesson, 3.9, focuses on precise words and phrases as transitions.

Patterns of Power **Lesson 13.3: Ink a Link: Using Adjectives After the Verb** focuses on using adjectives, but its model text aligns with our revision lesson on adding connecting ideas. Additionally, if you've been studying the apostrophe this year, you'll definitely want to highlight the abundance of apostrophes used throughout this model text: *Let Liberty Rise! How America's Schoolchildren Helped Save the Statue of Liberty.*

Setting the Context

Chana Stiefel's *Let Liberty Rise! How America's Schoolchildren Helped Save the Statue of Liberty* tells the story of how a community of everyday Americans, including thousands of school children, came together to purchase and construct a pedestal for the Statue of Liberty to stand upon. Share this information with your students if you've haven't already read the book to them, and then read aloud the following excerpt (with a missing sentence that you will reveal later).

It was an enormous statue—one of the largest the world was yet to see! With her torch held high, she was a symbol of freedom and friendship between two countries.

Invite students to consider how this paragraph is written and the meaning within it. "Guess what? A sentence is missing from this paragraph. Did you notice? Are you left wondering anything? Does anything seem unclear?"

When the conversation warrants, share what writers do to clear up confusions their readers may have: "Writers add sentences to connect ideas and clear up any confusion for their readers."

 Revision Strategy

Add a sentence to connect one idea to the next.

Modeling

Display **3.8 Something's Missing: Part I**, which has a mentor paragraph that shows where a new transitional sentence needs to be inserted. "The writer of this paragraph needs to revise by adding a sentence that will connect ideas for the reader. Let's look at this paragraph in which something's missing." Discuss the author's message in the existing parts around the blank. You may choose to use the author's first name within these questions to prompt discussion:

- What is Chana saying in the first sentence? What about the sentence after the blank?
- What is Chana's message in this paragraph?
- What do you notice about the writing before/after the blank space?

Invite students to consider which of the three starred sentence choices could be added to the author's writing. Model trying out one of the sentences, reading it in the paragraph, and discussing WHY this option works or doesn't seem to work well. Continue to model with the other two starred options or invite students to try it out and discuss in pairs or small groups. Remind students that their conversation should focus on WHY the author might choose or not choose to add the sentence rather than trying to select the right answer. After some time for conversation about the meaning and effect of each choice, reveal the author's original version with the display page **3.8 Something's Missing: Part II**. Use the reflective questions to guide a comparative analysis discussion.

- Why do you think the author used this sentence?
- Do any of the other starred sentence options work? Why or why not?
- Why do you think your choice was different from or the same as the author's?

Collaborating Through Conversation

Display **3.8 Invitation to Add Connectors: Part I**. In pairs or small groups, students collaborate through conversation with their peers to select the sentence they think best connects the information for the reader (Figure 3.8). While working, remind students to focus their conversation on meaning and effect: what works, what doesn't, and why. When ready, students compare their revision with others in class, discussing WHY they made their choices. To close the discussion, display **3.8 Invitation to Add Connectors Part II** to show the author's original text for comparative analysis and use the reflective questions to facilitate a further conversation about meaning and effect.

Applying Revision

Students return to a piece of writing they have drafted and use Chana Stiefel's choices as mentors for revision. You may have them start with a partner, sharing their goal for the piece: "As a reader, I want you to understand or get _____ from this piece." They then read their selection and ask their partner to help find a part that might be a little confusing or needs more connecting information added. Some questions their partner may ask include:

- What are you saying in the first sentence?
- What is your message in this part?
- What do you want your reader to know here?

After this conference with a partner, the writer can decide how they will insert a sentence or more to connect information or clear up any confusion. If time permits, invite them to meet back with their partner for another check with the revisions in place.

Sharing Results

Figure 3.8

Third graders discuss which sentence to add to Chana Stiefel's paragraph during the collaboration conversation part of the lesson.

Celebrate the revision writers did in this lesson with a small-group share. Students number off and meet up with other students that have the same number to form groups. Students name something they noticed another writer do to revise their piece for coherence such as "I noticed you added a sentence that connected _____. This helped me as a reader because _____."

3.8
Something's Missing: Part I

It was an enormous statue—one of the largest the world was yet to see!

With her torch held high, she was a symbol of freedom and friendship between two countries.

 Her name was Liberty.

 It was America's 100th Birthday!

 One month later, the Statue of Liberty arrived at New York's Bedloe's Island.

3.8
Something's Missing: Part II

The bolded sentence below is Chana Stiefel's sentence choice for adding a connecting idea in *Let Liberty Rise! How America's Schoolchildren Helped Save the Statue of Liberty.*

It was an enormous statue—one of the largest the world was yet to see! **Her name was Liberty.** With her torch held high, she was a symbol of freedom and friendship between the two countries.

Reflective Questions for Meaning and Effect

- Why do you think the author used this sentence?

- Do any of the other starred sentence options work? Why or why not?

- Why do you think your choice was different from or the same as the author's?

We study authors' choices, not because they're the only answer, but because they are an option. Writers need options.

3.8

Invitation to Add Connectors: Part I

In *Let Liberty Rise! How America's Schoolchildren Helped Save the Statue of Liberty*, the author explains what happens once the Statue of Liberty is put together.

- Read the paragraph on the next page.

- Study what the paragraph is mainly describing.

- Look closely at the sentences before the blank as well as the ones after the blank.

- Study the three starred sentences.

- Try each starred sentence in the blank and decide which one makes the most sense.

- Compare your version with other groups or pairs.

- Compare and contrast your version with the author's original text.

3.8

Invitation to Add Connectors: Part I *(continued)*

There she stood, tall and proud, the Statue of Liberty, America's symbol of freedom and hope.

Holding her torch high, the Statue of Liberty welcomed them to their new home.

 A parade passed by Pulitzer's *World* building.

 After the celebrations, steamships carrying new immigrants sailed into New York Harbor.

 Once the pedestal was finished, Lady Liberty was freed from her crates.

3.8

Invitation to Add Connectors: Part II

Original Text from *Let Liberty Rise! How America's Schoolchildren Helped Save the Statue of Liberty*

The bolded sentence below is Chana Stiefel's sentence choice for adding a connecting idea in *Let Liberty Rise! How America's Schoolchildren Helped Save the Statue of Liberty.*

There she stood, tall and proud, the Statue of Liberty, America's symbol of freedom and hope. **After the celebrations, steamships carrying new immigrants sailed into New York Harbor.** Holding her torch high, the Statue of Liberty welcomed them to their new home.

Reflective Questions for Meaning and Effect

• Why do you think the author used this sentence?

• Do any of the other starred sentence options work? Why or why not?

• Why do you think your choice was different from or the same as the author's?

We study authors' choices, not because they're the only answer, but because they are an option. Writers need options.

3.9 Cat Got Your Transition?

Lesson Overview

Revision goal connected to standards:

Develop and strengthen writing by connecting ideas with precise words, phrases, and transitions.

Model Text

The Cat Man of Aleppo
- – Written by Irene Latham and Karim Shamsi-Basha
- – Illustrated by Yuko Shumizu

Teacher Considerations

Now that students have had a chance to think about how ideas connect for coherence and clarity, they can narrow things down even more to choose precise words or phrases that help connect and transition from idea to the next. Beyond the familiar time-order transition words, we also want to keep in mind that the use of adjectives, adverbs, and prepositions can act as pathways for transitioning and connecting. We might use words and phrases to show time, location, or order. We can also use words and phrases to emphasize an idea or to compare or contrast two ideas. Another way we use transitions is to provide additional information or to summarize ideas (see **Writers Connect Ideas and Link to the Next with Transitions chart** on page 114). In this lesson, we use the model text, *The Cat Man of Aleppo*, to show how writers use precise words or phrases to connect ideas to transition from one idea to the next. Although we provide a chart of possible words and phrases to use, the options really are endless, so you will not find the word choices the authors of this book made on our chart. What you will find on this chart are some common ways writers connect their ideas or transition from one to the next. We suggest students use this chart as a starting place or a guide and then think beyond it as they start to collect words or phrases that can best show the connection between their ideas and why.

Writers Connect Ideas and Link to the Next with Transitions

Words and Phrases You Might Use

To Show Time or Order		To Show Location	
first	meanwhile	beyond	by
soon	now	on top of	inside
after	as soon as	throughout	within

To Compare Ideas		To Contrast Ideas	
in the same way	like	however	unlike
similarly	also	instead	bigger than
likewise	accordingly	although	on the other hand

To Emphasize an Idea		To Provide More Information	
indeed	in fact	additionally	for example
specifically	with this in mind	also	another
again	anyway	furthermore	and

To Summarize Ideas			
in conclusion	as a result	therefore	consequently

Setting the Context

Patterns of Power Lesson 15.3: Sooner or Later: Adverbs of Time connects nicely to this revision lesson, or you may consider guiding your students to think more about using precise words to compare and contrast with the *Patterns of Power* lessons in Chapter 14 on comparatives and superlatives.

In the Caldecott Honor–winning true story, *The Cat Man of Aleppo,* Irene Latham and Karim Shamsi-Basha share how Mohammad Alaa Aljaleel provided safety and love to his town's abandoned cats during the Syrian civil war.

As with the other Invitation to Add Connectors lessons, hold off initially on letting your students know that we've removed a sentence from the following text excerpt. Read the excerpt to set a context for this lesson, keeping in mind you'll reveal the original version later.

"Taee, atta atta," Alaa calls. *Here, kitty kitty*. A dozen cats rush toward him, their tails high. He gives them bits of meat and talks softly to them. The cats chew and purr, purr and chew. He smiles and pets the cats, and they love him back.

Now share with your students. "Guess what? A sentence is missing from this paragraph. Although these sentences seem to go together, we could probably make things clearer by adding a sentence that uses precise words or phrases to transition from one idea to another."

Revision Strategy
Add a transitional sentence using precise words
or phrases to move from one idea to another.

Modeling

Display **3.9 Something's Missing: Part I**, which has a mentor paragraph that shows where a new transitional sentence needs to be added in. "The writers of this paragraph need to revise by adding a transitional sentence. Let's look at this paragraph in which something's missing." Discuss the authors' message in the existing parts around the blank. Possible questions to prompt discussion:

- What are the authors showing in the first few sentences?
- What is the authors' message in the sentence that follows the blank?
- What do you notice about the writing before/after the blank space?

Students consider the three starred sentence options on the display page and think about which could be added to make the authors' writing clearer. Model trying out one of the sentences, reading it in the paragraph, talking it out, and discussing WHY it works or doesn't work well. Guide the conversation as students work to find precise words or phrases that support meaning and effect rather than right or wrong answers. Continue to model with the other two starred options or invite the writers to try it out together and discuss in pairs or small groups. When ready, share the original version of the excerpt for further discussion, using the display page **3.9 Something's Missing: Part II**, considering the following guiding questions together.

- Why do you think the authors used this sentence?
- Do any of the other starred sentence options work? Why or why not?
- Why do you think your choice was different from or the same as the authors'?

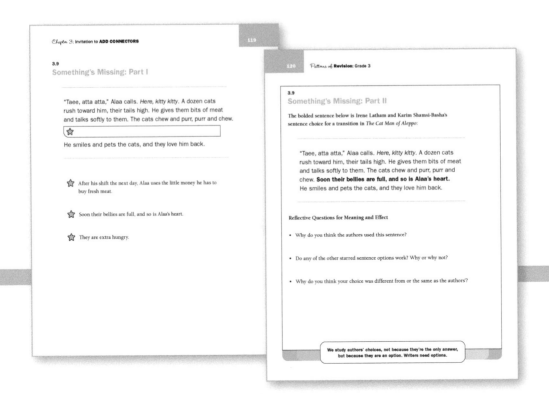

Collaborating Through Conversation

Display **3.9 Invitation to Add Connectors: Part I**. In pairs or small groups, students follow the directions on the display page to collaborate through conversation with one or more classmates, selecting the sentence they think best transitions to a new idea and should be added to the paragraph. Remind them to discuss how the writer is moving from one connected point to the next, using the chart from this lesson as a guide. This conversation is about what works, what doesn't work, and why. It's not about who is right and who is wrong. When ready, students compare their transitional sentence choice with others in class, discussing WHY they made their choice as opposed to the other sentences. Finally, using **3.9 Invitation to Add Connectors: Part II**, share the authors' original text for comparative analysis and use the reflective questions at the bottom of the display page to facilitate a concluding conversation about meaning and effect.

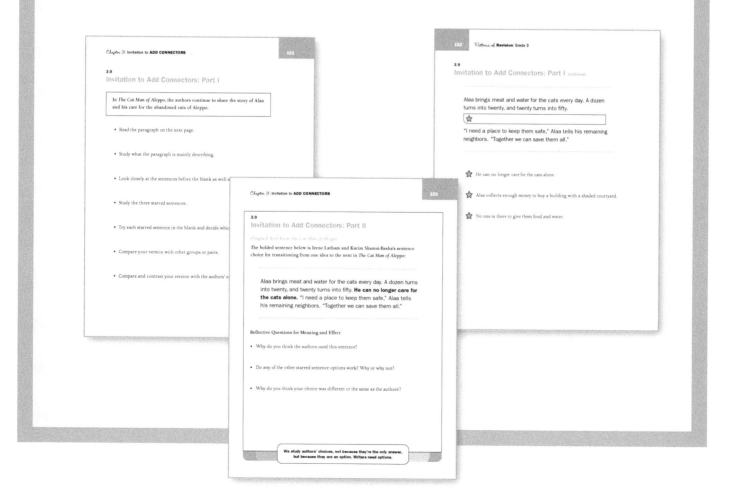

Considering Irene Latham and Karim Shamsi-Basha as mentors for adding connectors, revisit a class-created draft together, using the chart from page 114 to make decisions about which words, phrases, or sentences could be added to connect. Then students return to their own piece of writing they have drafted. Invite them to choose one section to focus on, using the chart as a guide to think about how they can add transitional sentences, phrases or words. Students add their transitional sentences using a carat, a sticky note, or a strip of paper taped onto their piece. Then, invite them to look at their entire piece, paying attention to how one paragraph transitions or links to the next. They may find that they are already using some precise words or phrases. If this is the case, invite them to highlight these words and use their chart to consider why they chose to use them, and then to see if they want to stick with those choices or revise them.

Possible prompts include:

- What did you show at the beginning of this part?
- What is your message that follows?
- How are your ideas connected?
- What might you add to transition from one idea to another? Why?

If time permits, students can continue this revision practice in another part of their writing or even in another piece.

Celebrate the revision writers did in this lesson with a partner share. Then choose one or two students to share with the whole class, naming how the writer used the revision strategy of adding a transition using precise words, phrases, or a sentence to move from one idea to another. Use the chart from this lesson to help writers name how and why they chose to use words or phrases.

3.9

Something's Missing: Part I

"Taee, atta atta," Alaa calls. *Here, kitty kitty*. A dozen cats rush toward him, their tails high. He gives them bits of meat and talks softly to them. The cats chew and purr, purr and chew.

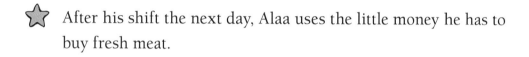

He smiles and pets the cats, and they love him back.

 After his shift the next day, Alaa uses the little money he has to buy fresh meat.

 Soon their bellies are full, and so is Alaa's heart.

 They are extra hungry.

3.9
Something's Missing: Part II

The bolded sentence below is Irene Latham and Karim Shamsi-Basha's sentence choice for a transition in *The Cat Man of Aleppo*:

"Taee, atta atta," Alaa calls. *Here, kitty kitty*. A dozen cats rush toward him, their tails high. He gives them bits of meat and talks softly to them. The cats chew and purr, purr and chew. **Soon their bellies are full, and so is Alaa's heart.** He smiles and pets the cats, and they love him back.

Reflective Questions for Meaning and Effect

• Why do you think the authors used this sentence?

• Do any of the other starred sentence options work? Why or why not?

• Why do you think your choice was different from or the same as the authors'?

> **We study authors' choices, not because they're the only answer, but because they are an option. Writers need options.**

3.9

Invitation to Add Connectors: Part I

> In *The Cat Man of Aleppo*, the authors continue to share the story of Alaa and his care for the abandoned cats of Aleppo.

- Read the paragraph on the next page.

- Study what the paragraph is mainly describing.

- Look closely at the sentences before the blank as well as the ones after the blank.

- Study the three starred sentences.

- Try each starred sentence in the blank and decide which one makes the most sense.

- Compare your version with other groups or pairs.

- Compare and contrast your version with the authors' original text.

(continues)

3.9

Invitation to Add Connectors: Part I *(continued)*

Alaa brings meat and water for the cats every day. A dozen turns into twenty, and twenty turns into fifty.

"I need a place to keep them safe," Alaa tells his remaining neighbors. "Together we can save them all."

 He can no longer care for the cats alone.

 Alaa collects enough money to buy a building with a shaded courtyard.

 No one is there to give them food and water.

3.9

Invitation to Add Connectors: Part II

Original Text from *The Cat Man of Aleppo*

The bolded sentence below is Irene Latham and Karim Shamsi-Basha's sentence choice for transitioning from one idea to the next in *The Cat Man of Aleppo*:

Alaa brings meat and water for the cats every day. A dozen turns into twenty, and twenty turns into fifty. **He can no longer care for the cats alone.** "I need a place to keep them safe," Alaa tells his remaining neighbors. "Together we can save them all."

Reflective Questions for Meaning and Effect

- Why do you think the authors used this sentence?

- Do any of the other starred sentence options work? Why or why not?

- Why do you think your choice was different or the same as the authors'?

We study authors' choices, not because they're the only answer, but because they are an option. Writers need options.

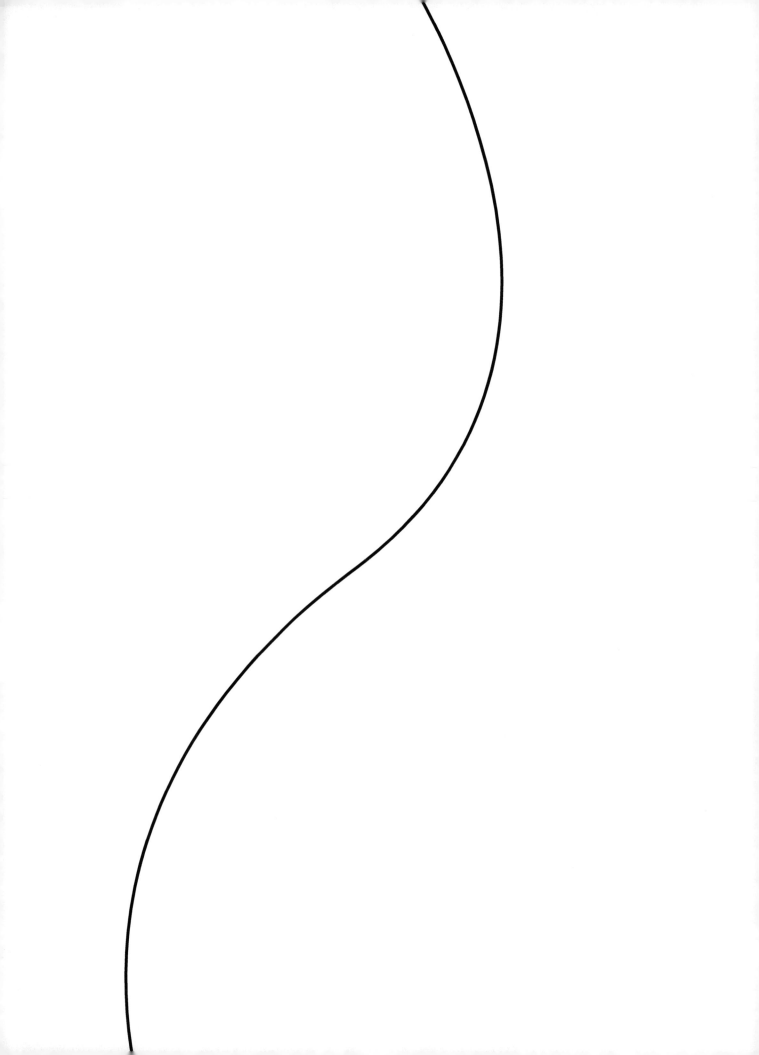

REVISION
Through Sentence
COMBINING

Part 2
Putting **DRAFT** Together

Teachers are often told to teach writing strategies, including those regarding revision, within context, but what does that mean exactly?

In the context of literacy, our students need to write, read, talk, and think. In Part 2, students continue learning what writers do by exploring and examining texts written by published authors—texts they are already reading or want to read. But, at this point, we're ready to level up those conversations as students try out the moves they've learned in earlier lessons in a cumulative way, combining ideas, sentences, words, and phrases while considering the best revisions for the message they are trying to convey. And, as they've done in every lesson up to this point, students will continue to talk through their choices with each other as they think about meaning and effect in their writing.

The lessons in Part 2 offer a culmination of all the revision strategies we've introduced so far and are grounded in a powerful mnemonic—**DRAFT** (delete, rearrange, add connectors, form new verbs, and talk it out; page 130)—to remind young writers of their options when revising. Notice, in this mnemonic, how the critical conversations we've centered student learning on across the lessons so far find a prominent placement, rounding things out as the final component—**T** for *talk*. The ten sentence-combining lessons that follow give third-grade writers additional application opportunities through larger, more open, interpretive experimentation to apply both what they intuitively know and the patterns of revision targeted structures they've encountered in earlier lessons.

As you move into the second part of this book and its lessons, recognize that—at least initially—things could get messy. Take a close look at children who play with something for the first time—a toy, a video game, something that has to be put together. They mess around with it, trying it out in different ways to see what works. They learn to use the toy effectively, learn to play the game effectively, learn to build the model effectively. But this all comes after several starts and stops, messy mistakes, and realizations that only come with hands-on exploration.

Through this play, this trial and error, comes effectiveness.

And, in this same way, our writers will find success through the play they do with revision. Remember, writing is a process. Revision is part of that process. The most important thing we can do when teaching students to combine sentences is to resist the urge to fix and, instead, embrace the play involved in revising, helping students see the choices they have as writers. We celebrate the experimentation, the discovery, and the approximations that may or may not also come with errors.

> 66 We celebrate the experimentation, the discovery, and the approximations that may or may not also come with errors. 99

As we always say, "Mistakes are a sign of growth." When learning something new, we have to try it out and even fail a few times before we get comfortable with it. It's not always correct, but it gets better and more effective over time. Inviting students to try combining sentences in multiple ways allows them to discover how some decisions make more meaning and have a stronger effect on the reader than others. This creates a flexible mindset, space for risk taking, and a pathway to a stronger craft of writing. So as students play with the choices they have as writers, relax. Breathe in the value of what they are doing. Trust where it will lead them.

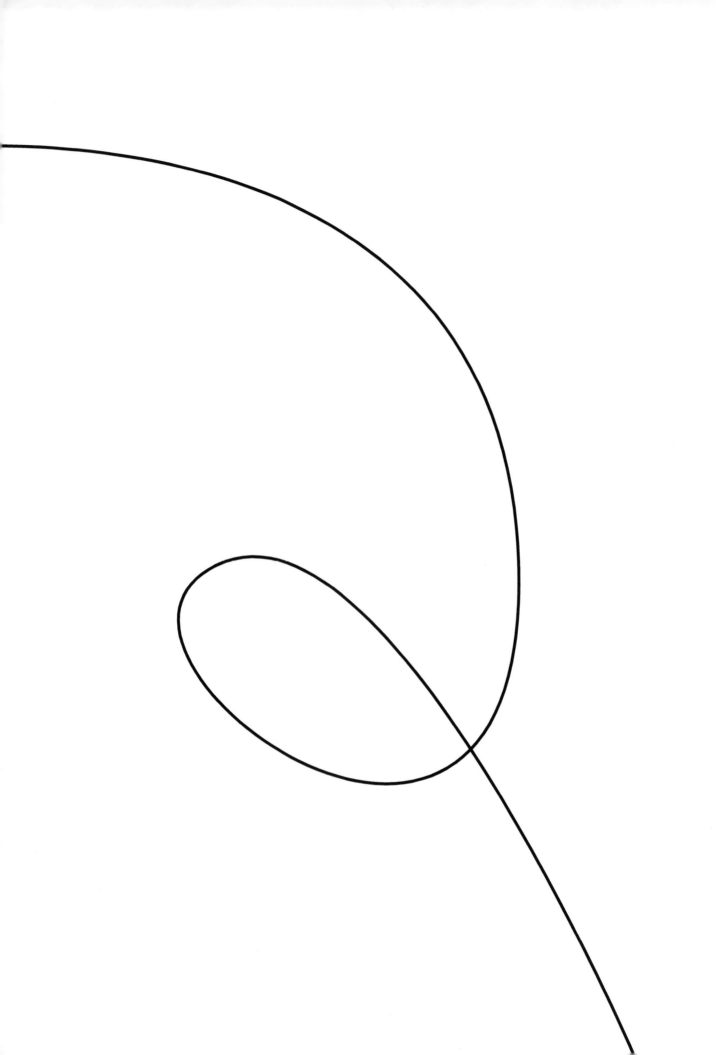

4
Invitation to
COMBINE

Read, read, read. Read everything . . . classics, good and bad, and see how they do it.
Just like a carpenter who works as an apprentice and studies the master. Read! You'll absorb it.
Then write. If it's good, you'll find out. If it's not, throw it out of the window.

– William Faulkner

ow that students have been introduced to the revision strategies of deleting, rearranging, adding, and talking it out, we use the largest of the lesson sets in this final chapter to give them practice applying the DRAFT mnemonic as a cumulative process to support sentence combining to revise.

We also use these lessons to touch on the **F** in DRAFT: *Form new verbs*—but purposefully do so with a light touch. Verbs are where the action is. Wielding them effectively requires a certain degree of finesse. When combining sentences or ideas, writers will sometimes need to change the verb endings or form new verbs to match the structure of the revised sentence. Although this level of sophistication may exceed the know-how of most third-grade writers, you might have some that show you they are ready to play with this use of language and sentence structure. If so, we invite you to grab the **Form New Verbs chart** for the fourth grade (available at www.routledge.com/9781625316318) and explore this more advanced concept with these particular writers during individual conferences or small-group writing lessons. Though we don't include explicit lessons for *form new verbs* in this chapter, we do dip into it conversationally in Lesson 3.18 when we change the verb to the infinitive. But this doesn't mean writers need to wait until Lesson 3.18 to notice the **F** on their **DRAFT Reviser's Dashboard chart**. In each lesson leading up to it, discuss the possibility of changing the verbs as you talk out the process of combining sentences. This will prepare third graders for deeper levels of sophistication when they're called to use this strategy in fourth grade and beyond.

The sentence-combining lessons in this chapter are fertile ground for students to refine their skill of making choices and then evaluating them for effect. Expect students to do a lot of *talking it out* in every lesson in this chapter, like all the ones before it. More options can lead to more sharing, which in turn exposes writers to more possibilities and their effects. By this time, students know there isn't one right answer but, rather, options that work better (or not).

All the lessons in this chapter follow the same format. We share several sentences that have been pulled by deconstructing the model sentence. First, we use DRAFT to discuss how we could combine the ideas into one sentence, then writers try out a different set of sentences in small groups or with partners. As with other lessons in this book, we conclude each interaction by inviting students to go back to their own writing, this time considering how they could combine some ideas to make their piece more concise and effective. And, as always, we encourage lots of time for sharing out loud and celebrating others' versions to deepen the students' understanding.

REVISER'S DRAFTboard

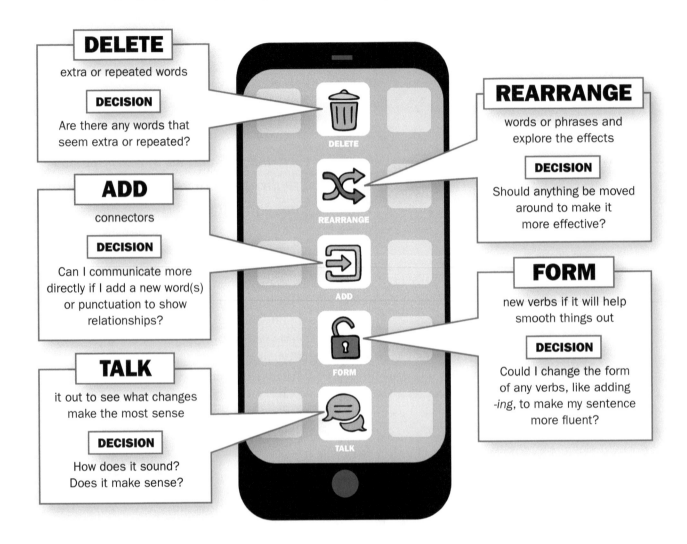

DELETE

extra or repeated words

DECISION

Are there any words that seem extra or repeated?

ADD

connectors

DECISION

Can I communicate more directly if I add a new word(s) or punctuation to show relationships?

TALK

it out to see what changes make the most sense

DECISION

How does it sound? Does it make sense?

REARRANGE

words or phrases and explore the effects

DECISION

Should anything be moved around to make it more effective?

FORM

new verbs if it will help smooth things out

DECISION

Could I change the form of any verbs, like adding *-ing*, to make my sentence more fluent?

3.10 The Art and Architecture of DRAFT

Lesson Overview

Revision goal connected to standards:

Develop and strengthen writing by combining ideas to avoid redundancy, add clarity, and improve fluency.

Model Text

Dream Builder: The Story of Architect Philip Freelon
- Written by Kelly Starling Lyons
- Illustrated by Laruen Freeman

Teacher Considerations

With this lesson, we begin revisiting the various ways students have learned to revise and how we can use these same strategies collectively to better combine our ideas and sentences. Behind the scenes, we have taken a sentence from Kelly Starling Lyons's *Dream Builder: The Story of Architect Philip Freelon* and deconstructed it into several separate sentences. Invite young writers to consider the sentences as they move through the DRAFT Reviser's Dashboard, looking for ways they can revise the collection into one sentence that shows a list, using the serial comma. Since this lesson also introduces DRAFT, you'll notice that we include more teacher guidance here than the other lessons in this chapter. You may choose to display the DRAFT Reviser's Dashboard or have students glue it into their notebooks. (See chart on page 130.) Keep in mind that you might casually recognize **F**, form new verbs, on the DRAFT Reviser's Dashboard as another strategy that can be—but isn't always—used. As it comes up, invite your writers to consider it conversationally, and enjoy the discussion as they play around with the possibilities it presents, but recall that most of the combining lessons in third grade will not lend themselves to forming new verbs.

Patterns of Power **Lesson 19.1: Catalogue a Frog: Items in a List** and **Lesson 19.2: Whatever Rings Your Smell: Items in a List** focus on using commas in a series, giving your students continued learning with this combining strategy.

Setting the Context

In *Dream Builder: The Story of Architect Philip Freelon*, Kelly Starling Lyons shares the story of the life of Philip Freelon and how he grew up to become the designer of the Smithsonian National Museum of African American History and Culture. To set a context for combining sentences in this lesson, read aloud this excerpt from *Dream Builder: The Story of Architect Philip Freelon*:

Philip hears birds crooning and squirrels scampering across crunchy leaves. He smells the fragrance of the earth. He feels the breeze dance across his honey skin.

Phil is seeing the world with an artist's inner eye.

As Phil grows older, his special sight deepens.

Then share with your students, "Here we learn a little about Philip Freelon. The author, Kelly Starling Lyons, has more to share with us about him, and she has done so through a combination of sentences. Writers often take short sentences or ideas with repetitive information and combine them into one."

Display the **DRAFT Reviser's Dashboard chart**, showing the DRAFT mnemonic, or distribute individual copies to each student, inviting them to glue it in their notebook.

"Writers, we have learned the revision strategies of deleting, rearranging, and adding and have considered how these can help us make our writing stronger. Today, we are going to use those same strategies together as we think about how we can combine some sentences or ideas. Take a look at this chart. When we discover that we have several ideas or sentences that go together, but seem a little redundant as separate sentences, we can make it more concise by combining. To do this, we can use DRAFT. We first look to see if there are any words or phrases that are repeated, and we think about deleting them. Then, we rearrange the words we have left to see how they might go together in one sentence. At this point, we will probably discover that we need to add something to connect the ideas, like words or phrases, or even punctuation marks, like commas. As we do this, we form a new sentence, which means we might also need to form new words by changing the verb endings to help smooth out the sentence. And as always, we talk it out, playing with several options to see what is the most effective. Let's use this chart together to combine some ideas from *Dream Builder: The Story of Architect Philip Freelon*."

 Revision Strategy   Use DRAFT to combine ideas and sentences.

Modeling

Use the DRAFT Reviser's Dashboard, along with printable **3.10 Modeled Sentence Combo: Part I**, to explore the three sentences that need to be combined into one. "There are three sentences here about Philip Freelon as an older child. Let's use our DRAFT Reviser's Dashboard and see if we can make these three sentences into one, like Kelly Starling Lyons did. First let's read aloud the sentences":

His thoughts have color.

His thoughts have shape.

His thoughts have form.

"Let's spend some time talking out ways we could combine these sentences, using any of the DRAFT strategies that help." Return to the DRAFT Reviser's Dashboard and work through its mnemonic as you model how to use DRAFT as a guide for combining the sentences. "D stands for *delete repetitive words*. Do you see some words that are repeated? Talk it out with a neighbor. What else do you see that is repeated?" Show students how to cross through "his thoughts have" in the second and third sentences (Figure 3.10).

Figure 3.10

3.10 Printable
Modeled Sentence Combo: Part I

His thoughts have color.

~~His thoughts have~~ shape.

~~His thoughts have~~ form.

(continues)

Modeling *(continued)*

"Now, how could we rearrange the words and add connectors?" Providing some ideas for possible connectors will help students talk through this combination. As a reminder, you may want to revisit **The Connectors chart** found on page 142.

Guide this conversation as you chart out some of their thoughts and model how to test their theories out for meaning and effect (talk it out).

Once the students feel like they have an effective combination, reveal the author's original sentence. Invite students to compare and contrast their version with Kelly's using **3.10 Modeled Sentence Combo: Part II**, prompting things along with the following reflective questions as necessary:

- Why do you think Kelly combined the sentences in this way?
- Is there another combination that would be effective?
- Why do you think your combination was different from or the same as Kelly's?
- If your combination was different from Kelly's, which do you prefer, and why?

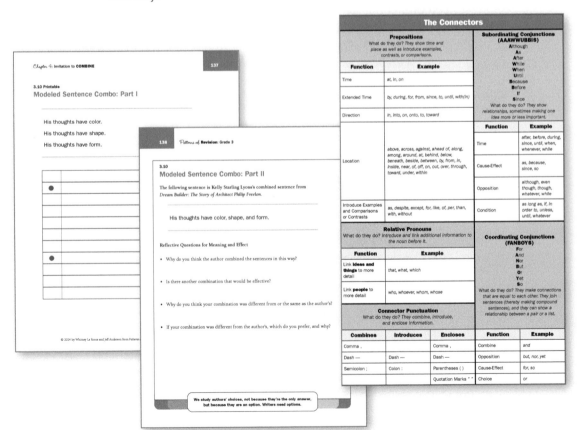

Collaborating Through Conversation

Distribute the printable **3.10 Invitation to Combine: Part I** to each student. Following the directions on the printable and using DRAFT, students collaborate through conversation with one or more classmates to combine the sentences into one. Invite them to record their possibilities on the lines provided on the printable. When ready, students compare their choices with other partnerships or groups. For comparative analysis, use the display page **3.10 Invitation to Combine: Part II** to share the author's original text. Use the reflective questions at the bottom of the display page to facilitate a conversation about meaning and effect.

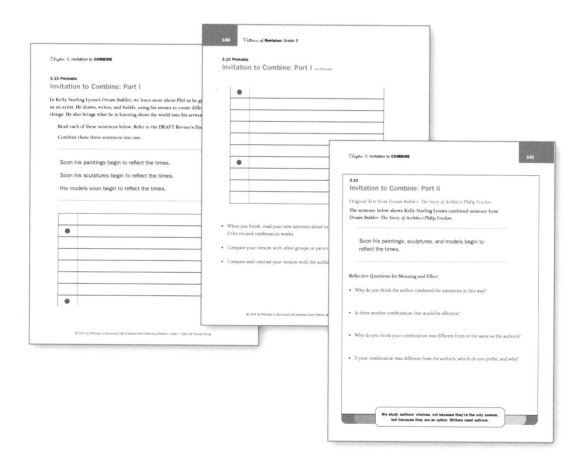

Applying Revision

Students return to their own writing to play with different sentence combos, using the DRAFT strategies and noticing the different effects. If they have a hard time finding sentences in their own writing to combine, invite them to create a practice box for combining their thinking. A box can be drawn directly onto the page or it can be added in as a sticky note. Students think about two or three additional things they want their reader to know and combine those thoughts into one sentence. For example, they may choose to write a sentence about the setting or the character if they are writing narrative. Or if they are writing an informational piece, they might write an additional sentence of combined ideas about the topic. If they choose, they can then work that new writing in somewhere in their piece, or they may not. If not, celebrate with them of the importance of trying on new and possible writing as part of the revision process—even if it doesn't work out.

Sharing Results

To celebrate, students share their combinations with a partner, demonstrating how they used DRAFT to combine their ideas into one sentence. Display their work by having them fold a piece of paper in half, horizontally, writing their original ideas on the top half with an arrow pointing down to the bottom half with their new combination.

3.10 Printable

Modeled Sentence Combo: Part I

His thoughts have color.

His thoughts have shape.

His thoughts have form.

3.10

Modeled Sentence Combo: Part II

The following sentence is Kelly Starling Lyons's combined sentence from
Dream Builder: The Story of Architect Philip Freelon.

His thoughts have color, shape, and form.

Reflective Questions for Meaning and Effect

• Why do you think the author combined the sentences in this way?

• Is there another combination that would be effective?

• Why do you think your combination was different from or the same as the author's?

• If your combination was different from the author's, which do you prefer, and why?

We study authors' choices, not because they're the only answer,
but because they are an option. Writers need options.

3.10 Printable

Invitation to Combine: Part I

In Kelly Starling Lyons's *Dream Builder*, we learn more about Phil as he grows as an artist. He draws, writes, and builds, using his senses to create different things. He also brings what he is learning about the world into his artwork.

Read each of these sentences below. Refer to the DRAFT Reviser's Dashboard.

Combine these three sentences into one:

Soon his paintings begin to reflect the times.

Soon his sculptures begin to reflect the times.

His models soon begin to reflect the times.

(continues)

3.10 Printable

Invitation to Combine: Part I *(continued)*

- When you finish, read your new sentence aloud to your group to see if the revised combination works.

- Compare your version with other groups or pairs in your class.

- Compare and contrast your version with the author's original text.

3.10

Invitation to Combine: Part II

Original Text from *Dream Builder: The Story of Architect Philip Freelon*

The sentence below shows Kelly Starling Lyons's combined sentence from
Dream Builder: The Story of Architect Philip Freelon:

Soon his paintings, sculptures, and models begin to reflect the times.

Reflective Questions for Meaning and Effect

- Why do you think the author combined the sentences in this way?

- Is there another combination that would be effective?

- Why do you think your combination was different from or the same as the author's?

- If your combination was different from the author's, which do you prefer, and why?

> We study authors' choices, not because they're the only answer,
> but because they are an option. Writers need options.

The Connectors

Prepositions
What do they do? *They show time and place as well as introduce examples, contrasts, or comparisons.*

Function	Example
Time	*at, in, on*
Extended Time	*by, during, for, from, since, to, until, with(in)*
Direction	*in, into, on, onto, to, toward*
Location	*above, across, against, ahead of, along, among, around, at, behind, below, beneath, beside, between, by, from, in, inside, near, of, off, on, out, over, through, toward, under, within*
Introduce Examples and Comparisons or Contrasts	*as, despite, except, for, like, of, per, than, with, without*

Subordinating Conjunctions (AAAWWUBBIS)
Although
As
After
While
When
Until
Because
Before
If
Since

What do they do? *They show relationships, sometimes making one idea more or less important.*

Function	Example
Time	*after, before, during, since, until, when, whenever, while*
Cause-Effect	*as, because, since, so*
Opposition	*although, even though, though, whatever, while*
Condition	*as long as, if, in order to, unless, until, whatever*

Relative Pronouns
What do they do? *Introduce and link additional information to the noun before it.*

Function	Example
Link **ideas and things** to more detail	*that, what, which*
Link **people** to more detail	*who, whoever, whom, whose*

Connector Punctuation
What do they do? *They combine, introduce, and enclose information.*

Combines	Introduces	Encloses
Comma ,		Comma ,
Dash —	Dash —	Dash —
Semicolon ;	Colon :	Parentheses ( )
		Quotation Marks " "

Coordinating Conjunctions (FANBOYS)
For
And
Nor
But
Or
Yet
So

What do they do? *They make connections that are equal to each other. They join sentences (thereby making compound sentences), and they can show a relationship between a pair or a list.*

Function	Example
Combine	*and*
Opposition	*but, nor, yet*
Cause-Effect	*for, so*
Choice	*or*

3.11 Drawing Things Together

Lesson Overview

Revision goal connected to standards:

Develop and strengthen writing by combining ideas to avoid redundancy, add clarity, and improve fluency.

Model Text

Drawing on Walls: A Story of Keith Haring
- Written by Matthew Burgess
- Illustrated by Josh Cochran

Teacher Considerations

We continue the heavy work of combining with this lesson, included to get students thinking about adverbs that tell time in addition to adding connector words, like *and*.

Still using DRAFT, we walk students through the act of combining ideas, ultimately composing a sentence with a compound predicate and beginning with an adverb showing time. As with all of the lessons in this section, we have taken an original sentence from the mentor text and deconstructed, or unrevised, it into several separate sentences. Through conversation, invite young writers to consider the sentences as they move through the DRAFT Reviser's Dashboard, looking for ways they can revise and combine them to create just one sentence. Expect a lot of talking it out throughout this work. As always, focus this revision talk on meaning and effect, rather than choosing a right answer.

Patterns of Power **Lesson 15.3: Sooner or Later: Adverbs of Time** gives students other examples of how authors use adverbs to show when, like Matthew Burgess does in *Drawing on Walls: A Story of Keith Haring* in this revision lesson.

Additionally, students learn about how authors use the serial comma and conjunctions to connect three or more actions in *Patterns of Power* **Lesson 19.3: Sisters, Brothers, or Friends: A Series of Things They Do.**

Setting the Context

In *Drawing on Walls: A Story of Keith Haring*, Matthew Burgess shares the story of Keith Haring's short life, honoring his art in public places and his connection with children. To set a context and introduce your students to Haring, who was born in Kutztown, Pennsylvania, read aloud the following excerpt from *Drawing on Walls*:

When Keith was 16, he began to feel restless in Kutztown.

That summer, he caught a bus to Ocean City, New Jersey, where he lived a block from the beach with kids from Pittsburgh and New York City.

Keith washed dishes to pay his way, and in his free time, he drew.

Then share with your students, "Matthew Burgess wants to share more information about Keith Haring. He chose to combine this information with multiple ideas about Keith into one sentence."

 Revision Strategy

Use DRAFT to combine ideas and sentences.

Modeling

Use the DRAFT Reviser's Dashboard, along with the printable **3.11 Modeled Sentence Combo: Part I**, to explore the three parts of the deconstructed original sentence that need to be combined into one. "There are three sentences here that show Matthew Burgess's ideas in Keith Haring's biography. Let's play around with revision and see if we can make these three sentences into one. First let's read aloud the sentences."

He would stay up all night.

He would watch the sunrise.

He would do these things sometimes.

Modeling *(continued)*

"Let's spend some time talking out ways we could combine these sentences, remembering that we can use any of the DRAFT strategies to help." Refer to the DRAFT Reviser's Dashboard as needed, walking through the steps for combining, saying things like, "I see the pronoun *he* three times. I'm sure I could revise this so there is only one pronoun *he*. Talk it out with a neighbor. What else do you see? How could you rearrange the words and add connectors?" Providing some ideas for possible connectors will help students to talk through this combination. (See **The Connectors** printable on page 142.)

Honor their variety of ways to combine the information, probing for clarity when necessary. You may also decide to remove the repetitious parts from each sentence, writing the leftover pieces on index cards to physically move the ideas around, guiding students through conversations about how to form the new sentence (Figure 3.11).

As students share, record some of their ideas in the space provided, modeling how we write down multiple versions, deciding which one is the most effective in the end. This conversation will show that writers have choices and that it is up to them to determine how their ideas should sound when read aloud.

Once the students feel like they have an effective combination, reveal the author's original sentence using the display page **3.11 Modeled Sentence Combo: Part II**. Invite students to compare and contrast their version with Matthew's, using the reflective questions as a guide:

- Why do you think Matthew combined the sentences in this way?
- Is there another combination that would be effective?
- Why do you think your combination was different from or the same as Matthew's?
- If your combination was different from Matthew's, which do you prefer, and why?

Figure 3.11

Collaborating Through Conversation

Distribute the printable **3.11 Invitation to Combine: Part I** to each student. Following the directions provided and using DRAFT, students collaborate through conversation with one or more classmates to combine the sentences into one. We've increased the number of sentences they are looking at when thinking about combining, so the conversation may take a little longer as students consider what is repeated and how the sentence might be rewritten. Remind students to use the workspace on the printable to write down their ideas, adding to them, and rewriting as they keep playing. Rather than erasing, have them write their new formation on the next line. This will leave evidence of the heavy work they do. When ready, students compare their choices with other partnerships or groups. Then, using the display page **3.11 Invitation to Combine: Part II**, share the author's original text for comparative analysis and use the reflective questions to facilitate a conversation about meaning and effect.

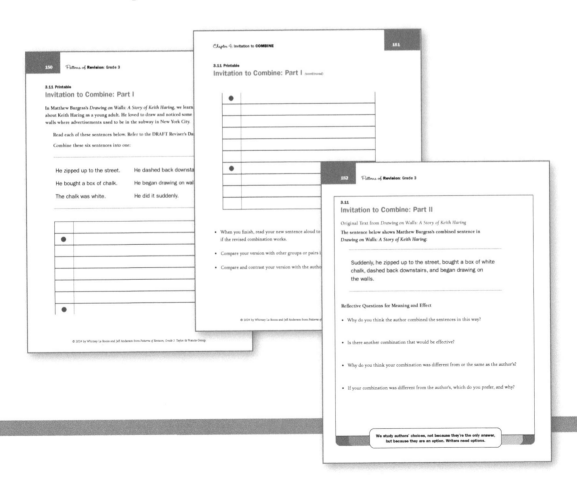

Applying Revision

Students return to their own writing, either a draft they are working on or anything in their writing notebook, to play with different sentence combinations, using the DRAFT strategies. Since this lesson uses the combination of one subject and multiple actions, invite students to look for places in their own writing where they find a subject doing multiple things and consider how they might combine those ideas into one sentence. Like the lesson before this, if students have a hard time finding sentences in their own writing to combine, invite them to create a practice box for combining their thinking. Then, they can insert that new writing somewhere in their piece.

You may also invite writers to consider adding adverbs that show when as an additional revision callback to previous lessons, while using this mentor text. Although this is a sentence-combining lesson, students can still revise using all of the strategies they've learned. Writers have options.

Sharing Results

Invite students to share and celebrate their revisions to music in a new way. Play some kid-friendly music while students wander the classroom. When the music stops, writers stop and share their revisions with someone near them, demonstrating how they used DRAFT to combine some of their ideas. When ready, play the music again for students to wander until the music stops for another chance to share with someone else. Repeat as often as you like!

3.11 Printable

Modeled Sentence Combo: Part I

He would stay up all night.

He would watch the sunrise.

He would do these things sometimes.

●	
●	

3.11

Modeled Sentence Combo: Part II

The following sentence is Matthew Burgess's combined sentence from
Drawing on Walls: A Story of Keith Haring:

Sometimes he would stay up all night and watch the sunrise.

Reflective Questions for Meaning and Effect

- Why do you think the author combined the sentences in this way?

- Is there another combination that would be effective?

- Why do you think your combination was different from or the same as the author's?

- If your combination was different from the author's, which do you prefer, and why?

We study authors' choices, not because they're the only answer,
but because they are an option. Writers need options.

3.11 Printable

Invitation to Combine: Part I

In Matthew Burgess's *Drawing on Walls: A Story of Keith Haring*, we learn more about Keith Haring as a young adult. He loved to draw and noticed some blank walls where advertisements used to be in the subway in New York City.

Read each of these sentences below. Refer to the DRAFT Reviser's Dashboard.

Combine these six sentences into one:

He zipped up to the street.   He dashed back downstairs.

He bought a box of chalk.   He began drawing on walls.

The chalk was white.   He did it suddenly.

3.11 Printable

Invitation to Combine: Part I *(continued)*

- When you finish, read your new sentence aloud to your group to see if the revised combination works.

- Compare your version with other groups or pairs in your class.

- Compare and contrast your version with the author's original text.

3.11

Invitation to Combine: Part II

Original Text from *Drawing on Walls: A Story of Keith Haring*

The sentence below shows Matthew Burgess's combined sentence in *Drawing on Walls: A Story of Keith Haring*:

Suddenly, he zipped up to the street, bought a box of white chalk, dashed back downstairs, and began drawing on the walls.

Reflective Questions for Meaning and Effect

- Why do you think the author combined the sentences in this way?

- Is there another combination that would be effective?

- Why do you think your combination was different from or the same as the author's?

- If your combination was different from the author's, which do you prefer, and why?

We study authors' choices, not because they're the only answer, but because they are an option. Writers need options.

3.12 **Dinner Time**

Lesson Overview

Revision goal connected to standards:

Develop and strengthen writing by combining ideas to avoid redundancy, add clarity, and improve fluency.

Model Text

A Different Pond
- – Written by Bao Phi
- – Illustrated by Thi Bui

Teacher Considerations

This lesson is designed for the continued use of DRAFT to combine without redundancy. Using the DRAFT Reviser's Dashboard, we will invite our students to delete repeated information, which is more than in the previous lessons. By adding connector words and considering rearranging of the prepositional phrases, students will discover how the use of DRAFT can help them be more concise and clear with their ideas.

Patterns of Power **Lessons 16.1, 16.2, and 16.3** give students opportunities to study the use of prepositional phrases and try using them in their own writing. Connecting this knowledge to how Bao Phi uses prepositional phrases in *A Different Pond* provides students another look at the placement of these phrases within sentences.

Additionally, your students may notice how Bao Phi uses the future tense in his writing. For a lesson on verb tense, check out *Patterns of Power* **Lesson 6.3: Have You Got the Time? Verb Tense.**

Setting the Context

In *A Different Pond*, a boy and his dad go fishing at night while finding value in spending the time together before his dad has to go to work. While Dad is at work, the boy thinks ahead to dinnertime, when the family will eat the fish he has caught. To set a context, read aloud this excerpt from Bao Phi's *A Different Pond* showing how the family will prepare dinner together:

> Tonight, when we are all home, Dad will put rice in the cooker, and Mom will fry the fish on both sides until they are crispy.

Now share with your students, "Next, the author wants to share what the boy will do to help prepare dinner. Let's take a look at these short sentences to see how we can combine them into one."

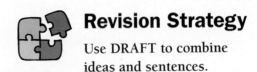

Revision Strategy

Use DRAFT to combine ideas and sentences.

Modeling

Use the printable **3.12 Modeled Sentence Combo: Part I** to explore the four sentences that together will be combined into one. "There are four sentences here that show Bao Phi's ideas in *A Different Pond*. Let's play around with revision using DRAFT and see if we can make these four sentences into one. First let's read aloud the sentences."

> I will bring out the fish sauce.
>
> The fish sauce has flecks of chili pepper floating on top.
>
> The fish sauce has carrots floating on top.
>
> The fish sauce is in a jar.

Modeling *(continued)*

"Let's spend some time talking out ways we could combine these sentences, remembering that we can use any of the DRAFT strategies that help." Review the DRAFT mnemonic as needed. Model how to combine the sentences, saying things like, "I'm noticing the words *fish sauce* in all four sentences. I don't think that is necessary. I'm sure I could revise this so *fish sauce* is used only once. Talk it out with a neighbor. What else do you see is repeated? How might we combine two of these sentences? How can we bring in the information from the other sentences to our combination? What connectors could we add?" Refer to **The Connectors** printable on page 142. You may choose to guide students to focus on the relative pronouns as connectors, linking ideas to more detail. As students share their ideas, record the thinking on the space provided on the printable, modeling how the jotting of a variety of combinations helps us decide how to form the sentence in the most effective way.

When the students feel like they have an effective combination, display the author's original sentence using the display page **3.12 Modeled Sentence Combo: Part II**. Engage students in conversation about how their combination and the original text are alike and different. Use the reflective questions as a guide:

- Why do you think Bao combined the sentences in this way?
- Is there another combination that would be effective?
- Why do you think your combination was different from or the same as Bao's?
- If your combination was different from Bao's, which do you prefer, and why?

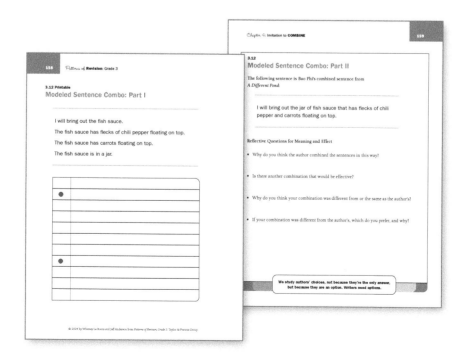

Collaborating Through Conversation

Distribute the printable **3.12 Invitation to Combine: Part I** to each student. Using DRAFT while following the directions on the printable, students collaborate through conversation with one or more classmates to combine the sentences into one. Invite them to really play around with the *Rearrange* part of DRAFT, moving phrases within their sentence around, writing down the newly formed sentences and talking them out to see which would be most effective. When ready, students compare their choices with others. Then, using the display page **3.12 Invitation to Combine: Part II**, share the author's original text for comparative analysis. Use the reflective questions at the bottom of the display page to facilitate a conversation about meaning and effect.

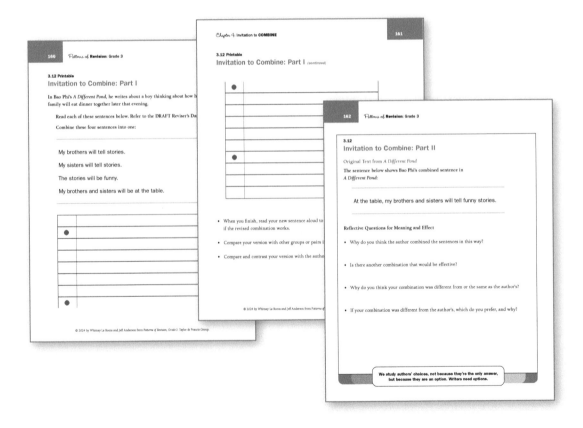

Applying Revision

Students return to their writer's notebook or a draft in their writing folder to play with different sentence combinations, using the DRAFT strategies (Figure 3.12). If reviewing the entire piece is overwhelming, invite students to choose one part, looking for repetition and ideas that could be combined. They may choose to add some prepositional phrases for detail and then move through DRAFT to see how to effectively combine their new ideas with their written ones. Students notice the different effects through this play. They may choose to use a relative pronoun from their **Connectors chart** like the word *that* to link ideas and things to more detail. If students need to use a practice box to practice combining thoughts or details that are not yet in their writing pieces, they can do that, too. This time is best spent in the act of combining sentences, details, or ideas.

Figure 3.12

This writer used DRAFT to combine some of his ideas about football.

Sharing Results

Using a large sheet of chart paper, create a graffiti board for students to post one of their combinations for others to see. As students share their combinations, invite them to point out how they used DRAFT to combine. Celebrate this revision by adding the strategy to the top of the graffiti board as a title: "Use DRAFT to Combine Sentences." Leave the board up for several days to extend the celebration.

3.12 Printable

Modeled Sentence Combo: Part I

I will bring out the fish sauce.

The fish sauce has flecks of chili pepper floating on top.

The fish sauce has carrots floating on top.

The fish sauce is in a jar.

3.12

Modeled Sentence Combo: Part II

The following sentence is Bao Phi's combined sentence from *A Different Pond*:

I will bring out the jar of fish sauce that has flecks of chili pepper and carrots floating on top.

Reflective Questions for Meaning and Effect

- Why do you think the author combined the sentences in this way?

- Is there another combination that would be effective?

- Why do you think your combination was different from or the same as the author's?

- If your combination was different from the author's, which do you prefer, and why?

We study authors' choices, not because they're the only answer, but because they are an option. Writers need options.

3.12 Printable

Invitation to Combine: Part I

In Bao Phi's *A Different Pond*, he writes about a boy thinking about how his family will eat dinner together later that evening.

Read each of these sentences below. Refer to the DRAFT Reviser's Dashboard.

Combine these four sentences into one:

My brothers will tell stories.

My sisters will tell stories.

The stories will be funny.

My brothers and sisters will be at the table.

●	
●	

3.12 Printable

Invitation to Combine: Part I *(continued)*

- When you finish, read your new sentence aloud to your group to see if the revised combination works.

- Compare your version with other groups or pairs in your class.

- Compare and contrast your version with the author's original text.

3.12

Invitation to Combine: Part II

Original Text from *A Different Pond*

The sentence below shows Bao Phi's combined sentence in
A Different Pond:

At the table, my brothers and sisters will tell funny stories.

Reflective Questions for Meaning and Effect

- Why do you think the author combined the sentences in this way?

- Is there another combination that would be effective?

- Why do you think your combination was different from or the same as the author's?

- If your combination was different from the author's, which do you prefer, and why?

We study authors' choices, not because they're the only answer,
but because they are an option. Writers need options.

3.13 There's More to Hair Than Meets the Eye

Lesson Overview

Revision goal connected to standards:

Develop and strengthen writing by combining ideas to avoid redundancy, add clarity, and improve fluency.

Model Text

J.D. and the Great Barber Battle
- Written by J. Dillard
- Illustrated by Akeem S. Roberts

Teacher Considerations

We continue the work of using DRAFT to combine ideas in this lesson with a little more depth and complexity, inviting students to envision what the ideas show in real life and how a writer could put those actions into a sentence. Like Lesson 3.11, students will ultimately compose sentences with compound predicates, but they will have to do more rearranging of words and ideas in this lesson. Talking it out will be key for students. Invite them to talk out what is happening in the sentences, envisioning the actions and the order of the actions, as they rearrange the words in the sentences and add connectors, creating an effective, fluent sentence.

Setting the Context

In *J.D. and the Great Barber Battle*, we are immediately introduced to J.D., the main character and narrator of the story. It is time for his haircut, and he has been checking out his friends' styles to get ideas for his own. J.D. admires cuts with designs worked in because he is an artist himself. To set a context, and to get to know J.D. a little more, read aloud this excerpt from Chapter 3 in J. Dillard's *J.D. and the Great Barber Battle*:

My art was award-winning. Once I got third in a competition for a sketch of a bass fish. It was still hanging up on a wall in the Meridian mall.

Now share with your students, "J.D. has more to say here. He can use short sentences to share the information, or he can combine them into one sentence."

Revision Strategy

Use DRAFT to combine ideas and sentences.

Modeling

Using the DRAFT Reviser's Dashboard, along with the printable **3.13 Modeled Sentence Combo: Part I**, explore the four sentences that together will be combined into one. "There are four sentences here that give us more information about J.D. Let's play around with revision and see if we can make these four sentences into one. First let's read aloud the sentences."

I started to draw pictures.

The pictures were of cartoons.

I drew pictures of comic book characters.

I pulled out my notebook.

Modeling *(continued)*

"Let's spend some time talking out ways we could combine these sentences, remembering that we can use any of the DRAFT strategies to help." Referring to the DRAFT Reviser's Dashboard as needed, walk through the steps for combining. You will most likely notice the repeating of the pronoun *I*. Invite students to help you see other repeated words. The conversation may lead to the use of the word *draw* and the word *drew*. At this point, invite students to visualize the actions in each sentence, and how they might fit together. Model jotting down a few different combinations, some using the word *draw* and some using the word *drew*. Which is more effective? Model rearranging the words and adding connectors. "We are visualizing two separate actions here, so we need to decide what connector word we could add to join the two actions in one sentence. What did J.D. do first? Then what?" Refer to **The Connectors chart** on page 142. You may discuss how you don't always need to form new verbs if what you have already works. DRAFT is a series of steps to help revise. There will be times when you use all of them and times when you will not. Writers have choices.

When ready, reveal the author's original version using the display page **3.13 Modeled Sentence Combo: Part II**. Compare and contrast the author's version to the class combination. Use the reflective questions as a guide:

- Why do you think J. Dillard combined the sentences in this way?
- Is there another combination that would be effective?
- Why do you think your combination was different from or the same as J. Dillard's?
- If your combination was different from J. Dillard's, which do you prefer, and why?

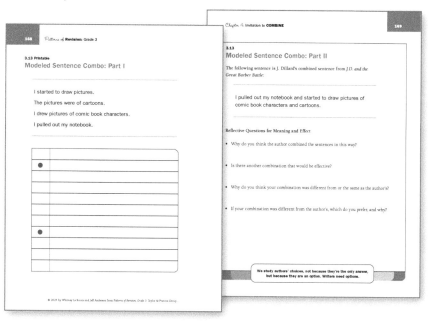

Collaborating Through Conversation

Distribute the printable **3.13 Invitation to Combine: Part I** to each student. Following directions on the printable while utilizing their DRAFT Reviser's Dashboard, students collaborate through conversation with one or more classmates to combine the sentences into one (Figure 3.13). Invite them to visualize the action in each sentence to help with ordering and rearranging. Remind students to use the workspace on the printable to write down their ideas, adding to them and rewriting as they keep playing. Rather than erasing, have them write their new formations on the next line, leaving evidence of the heavy work writers do during the revision process. When ready, students compare their choices with other partnerships or groups. Display **3.13 Invitation to Combine: Part II** to reveal the author's original version for comparative analysis. Use the reflective questions at the bottom of the display page to facilitate a conversation about meaning and effect.

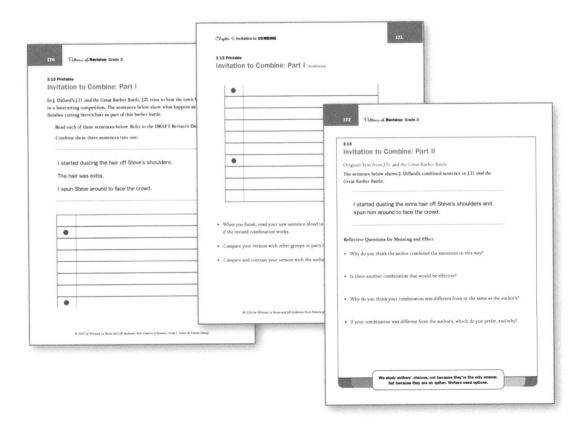

Applying Revision

Students return to their own writing to play with different sentence combinations, using the DRAFT strategies. It may be helpful for writers to invite a partner to help, reading their writing aloud, listening for repetition or ideas that could be combined. Some students may notice they haven't used any type of punctuation in their original writing, making this the perfect time to consider combining options, as they'll likely notice several ideas that may need to be revised into their own sentences or combined sentences—requiring some intentional punctuation work. Students notice the different effects and choose the combinations that provide the most clarity for the reader.

Figure 3.13

Working together during the collaboration conversation, students record their thinking and use the DRAFT strategies as they try out different combinations.

Sharing Results

Students share their revisions in small groups. Invite them to highlight their favorite combination and write why it is their favorite on a sticky note. For further celebration, hang the writing pieces with the attached sticky notes in the hallway so others can see the magic that happens with revision.

3.13 Printable

Modeled Sentence Combo: Part I

I started to draw pictures.

The pictures were of cartoons.

I drew pictures of comic book characters.

I pulled out my notebook.

●	
●	

3.13

Modeled Sentence Combo: Part II

The following sentence is J. Dillard's combined sentence from *J.D. and the Great Barber Battle*:

I pulled out my notebook and started to draw pictures of comic book characters and cartoons.

Reflective Questions for Meaning and Effect

- Why do you think the author combined the sentences in this way?

- Is there another combination that would be effective?

- Why do you think your combination was different from or the same as the author's?

- If your combination was different from the author's, which do you prefer, and why?

We study authors' choices, not because they're the only answer, but because they are an option. Writers need options.

3.13 Printable

Invitation to Combine: Part I

In J. Dillard's *J.D. and the Great Barber Battle*, J.D. tries to beat the town barber in a haircutting competition. The sentences below show what happens as J.D. finishes cutting Steve's hair as part of this barber battle.

Read each of these sentences below. Refer to the DRAFT Reviser's Dashboard.

Combine these three sentences into one:

I started dusting the hair off Steve's shoulders.

The hair was extra.

I spun Steve around to face the crowd.

3.13 Printable

Invitation to Combine: Part I *(continued)*

- When you finish, read your new sentence aloud to your group to see if the revised combination works.

- Compare your version with other groups or pairs in your class.

- Compare and contrast your version with the author's original text.

3.13

Invitation to Combine: Part II

Original Text from *J.D. and the Great Barber Battle*

The sentence below shows J. Dillard's combined sentence in *J.D. and the Great Barber Battle*:

I started dusting the extra hair off Steve's shoulders and spun him around to face the crowd.

Reflective Questions for Meaning and Effect

• Why do you think the author combined the sentences in this way?

• Is there another combination that would be effective?

• Why do you think your combination was different from or the same as the author's?

• If your combination was different from the author's, which do you prefer, and why?

We study authors' choices, not because they're the only answer, but because they are an option. Writers need options.

3.14 Read the Room

Lesson Overview

Revision goal connected to standards:

Develop and strengthen writing by combining ideas to avoid redundancy, add clarity, and improve fluency.

Model Text

Yasmin the Librarian
- Written by Saadia Faruqi
- Illustrated by Hatem Aly

Teacher Considerations

As we continue to invite students to use the DRAFT strategies to help them combine ideas and sentences, we use this lesson to also highlight adding an apostrophe to show possession when combining. We love the Yasmin series, and this book, *Yasmin the Librarian*, has several sentences that use possessive nouns while also demonstrating the use of descriptive word choice. Sometimes, students will add description to their writing with additional sentences. This lesson is used to show writers how they can use DRAFT to combine those additional sentences with sentences they already have in place to avoid redundancy.

 Patterns of Power **Lessons 9.1 and 9.2** provide students with more opportunities to explore examples of how authors use apostrophes to show possession.

Setting the Context

In Saadia Faruqi's *Yasmin the Librarian*, Yasmin gets to be a helper in the school library. To set a context, read aloud this excerpt from Chapter 1 of *Yasmin the Librarian*:

"Come in, come in!" called Mrs. Kogo, the librarian. "The library is waiting for you!"

The library was big and sunny. There were shelves and books everywhere.

Then share with your students, "Saadia Faruqi wants to add more description of the library for her readers. Let's see how we can take some of her ideas and combine them into one sentence."

 Revision Strategy

Use DRAFT to combine ideas and sentences.

Modeling

Use the DRAFT Reviser's Dashboard, along with the printable **3.14 Modeled Sentence Combo: Part I**, to model combining the ideas from Chapter 1 of *Yasmin the Librarian* into one. "These three sentences describe what Yasmin saw in the library. Let's play revision and see if we can combine these sentences into one. First let's read them aloud."

A pile of books was on the desk.

The desk belonged to Mrs. Kogo.

The pile was high.

Modeling *(continued)*

"Let's spend some time talking out ways we could combine these sentences, remembering that we can use any of the DRAFT strategies to help." Refer to the DRAFT Reviser's Dashboard as needed. When you approach the *A* for Add, invite students to talk this out, thinking about what punctuation could be added. Guide the conversation toward the use of the apostrophe, and model how to combine the ideas in the second sentence to write with a possessive noun, saying things like, "I see that the desk belonged to Mrs. Kogo. Maybe we can use a punctuation mark to write this in a different way. Let's use our Alphabetical Punctuation Guide to help us." See a printable of the **Alphabetical Punctuation Guide** on pages 183–184.

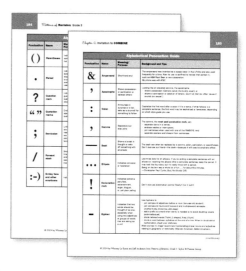

As you move through DRAFT, record a variety of possible combinations, showing students that writers play with words, punctuation, and sentences before arriving at a final choice. Once the students feel like they have an effective combination, reveal the author's original sentence using the display page **3.14 Modeled Sentence Combo: Part II**. Invite students to compare and contrast their version with Saadia's, using the reflective questions as a guide:

- Why do you think Saadia combined the sentences in this way?
- Is there another combination that would be effective?
- Why do you think your combination was different from or the same as Saadia's?
- If your combination was different from Saadia's, which do you prefer, and why?

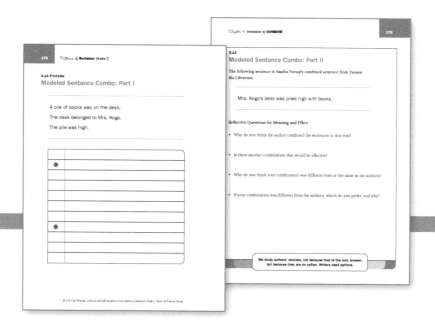

Collaborating Through Conversation

Distribute the printable **3.14 Invitation to Combine: Part I**, to each student. Following the directions provided and using DRAFT, students collaborate through conversation with one or more classmates to combine the sentences into one (Figure 3.14). Remind them to refer to the **Alphabetical Punctuation Guide** printable as needed. When ready, students compare their choices with others in the class. Then, using the display page **3.14 Invitation to Combine: Part II**, share the author's original text for comparative analysis. Use the reflective questions to facilitate a conversation about meaning and effect.

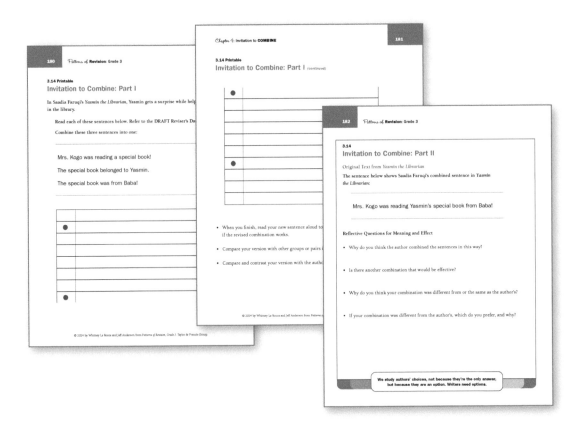

Applying Revision

Students return to their own writing, either a draft they are working on or anything in their writer's notebook, to play with different sentence combinations, using the DRAFT strategies. In addition to reading their piece to find possible places to combine, invite your students to also check for ownership, deciding if they need to delete some words, rearrange others, and add appropriate punctuation to show possession. They may discover ways to combine using other punctuation while referring to their **Alphabetical Punctuation Guide**. Allow for approximation during this process, asking about students about their choices—why and how they decided to make them. By explaining their thinking, writers show that they are the decision makers, and the choices they make are intentional.

Figure 3.14

Students work together with DRAFT to combine the sentences.

Sharing Results

Get students moving with this new way of sharing results of student revision. In each corner of the room, hang a piece of construction paper with one of the letters from DRAFT on it (*D* on one piece, *R* on another, and so on), excluding *T*. With your signal, students choose a corner and share how they used that part of DRAFT in their revision with the others in that group. Repeat to allow for students to move to another corner and share another way in which they used DRAFT, always talking out what they did to revise.

3.14 Printable

Modeled Sentence Combo: Part I

A pile of books was on the desk.

The desk belonged to Mrs. Kogo.

The pile was high.

●	
●	

3.14
Modeled Sentence Combo: Part II

The following sentence is Saadia Faruqi's combined sentence from *Yasmin the Librarian*:

Mrs. Kogo's desk was piled high with books.

Reflective Questions for Meaning and Effect

- Why do you think the author combined the sentences in this way?

- Is there another combination that would be effective?

- Why do you think your combination was different from or the same as the author's?

- If your combination was different from the author's, which do you prefer, and why?

We study authors' choices, not because they're the only answer, but because they are an option. Writers need options.

3.14 Printable

Invitation to Combine: Part I

In Saadia Faruqi's *Yasmin the Librarian*, Yasmin gets a surprise while helping in the library.

Read each of these sentences below. Refer to the DRAFT Reviser's Dashboard.

Combine these three sentences into one:

_____

Mrs. Kogo was reading a special book!

The special book belonged to Yasmin.

The special book was from Baba!

_____

3.14 Printable

Invitation to Combine: Part I *(continued)*

- When you finish, read your new sentence aloud to your group to see if the revised combination works.

- Compare your version with other groups or pairs in your class.

- Compare and contrast your version with the author's original text.

3.14

Invitation to Combine: Part II

Original Text from *Yasmin the Librarian*

The sentence below shows Saadia Faruqi's combined sentence in *Yasmin the Librarian*:

Mrs. Kogo was reading Yasmin's special book from Baba!

Reflective Questions for Meaning and Effect

- Why do you think the author combined the sentences in this way?

- Is there another combination that would be effective?

- Why do you think your combination was different from or the same as the author's?

- If your combination was different from the author's, which do you prefer, and why?

> **We study authors' choices, not because they're the only answer, but because they are an option. Writers need options.**

Alphabetical Puncuation Guide

Punctuation	Name	Meaning/Purpose	Background and Tips
&	**Ampersand**	Shorthand *and*	The ampersand was invented as a space saver in the 1700s and was used frequently for a time. Now its use is confined to names that contain it, such as A&W Root Beer or as a decoration. *My phone was with AT&T.*
'	**Apostrophe**	Shows possession or contraction or deleted letters	Looking like an elevated comma, the apostrophe: • shows possession (*Carlos's pencil, the book's cover*); or • shows a contraction or deletion of letters. (*Don't do that too often 'cause it sounds too casual.*)
:	**Colon**	Announces a surprise or a list; acts as a drumroll for something to follow	Capitalize the first word after a colon if it's a name; if what follows is a complete sentence, the first word may be capitalized or lowercase, depending on which style guide you use.
,	**Comma**	Separates but also joins	The comma, the **most used punctuation mark**, can • separate items in a series, • enclose asides or interrupters, • join sentences when used with one of the FANBOYS, and • separate openers and closers from sentences.
——	**Dash**	Shows a break in thought or sets off something with emphasis	The dash can often be replaced by a comma, colon, semicolon, or parentheses. Don't overuse our friend—the dash—because it will lose its emphatic effect.
• • •	**Ellipsis**	Indicates omission or hesitation	Use three dots for an ellipsis. If you're ending a complete sentence with an ellipsis or inserting the ellipsis after a complete sentence, keep the period. It may look like four dots, but it's really three with a period. *Being on the lam was a whole lot of fun . . . for about five minutes.* —Christopher Paul Curtis, *Bud, Not Buddy* (36)
!	**Exclamation mark**	Indicates extreme pain, fear, astonishment, anger, disgust, or just plain yelling	Don't overuse exclamation points! Really!! Cut it out!!!
-	**Hyphen**	Indicates that two words should be thought of as one, especially when using two adjectives or groups of words that are acting as a unit	Use hyphens to • join compound adjectives before a noun (*ten-year-old student*) • join compound nouns and two-word and multiple-word concepts (*mother-in-law, know-how, skin-deep*) • add a prefix to a word when clarity is needed or to avoid doubling vowels (*anti-intellectual*) • divide lettered words (*T-shirt, L-shaped, X-ray, U-turn*) • divide a word between syllables at the end of a line: *When in doubt about hyphen-ation, check your dictionary* *Most sources no longer recommend hyphenating proper nouns and adjectives relating to geography or nationality (Mexican American, Italian American).*

(continues)

Alphabetical Puncuation Guide *(continued)*

Punctuation	Name	Meaning/Purpose	Background and Tips
( )	**Parentheses**	Indicates an aside or something nonessential (parenthetical)	Parentheses may be used for • clarification of technical terms, • conversions or translations, and • asides.
.	**Period**	Indicates what the British call a "full stop." The sentence is over. Abbreviations and initials may also use periods.	*When you reach the period, it's all over.* —Patricia O'Conner, *Woe Is I* (134) *Mr. Chips, Ms. Pacman, Dr. Pepper, or gov.* No periods between initialisms such as CIA or NBA, or when a person's entire name is replaced with initials, such as JFK or RBG.
?	**Question mark**	Indicates, you guessed it, a question. It can also show doubt.	Need I say more? Genuine questions deserve their own mark. Don't use a question mark for indirect questions: *The principal is always asking me questions.*
" "	**Quotation marks**	Encloses direct speech or direct quotes from sources	*"Dialogue brings writing to life,"* said the student. (Use single quotation marks to indicate a quote within a quote.)
;	**Semicolon**	Links sentences with similar ideas. May be needed when there are already too many commas in a sentence.	Between the period and the comma lies the semicolon. When items in a series contain commas, separate them with a semicolon for clarity. Ships came and went; men and women did their chores, talked, and sought relief from the heat and insects; the markets and shops hummed with activity; children played; and the city, state, and federal governments went about their business. —Jim Murphy, *An American Plague* (9)
/	**Forward slash**	Shows the end of a line in quoted poetry and may be used to separate alternatives like either/or	Though the slash is used in legal documents, most mavens refrain from using it in prose, unless showing line endings in poetry. For example, dealing with the gender issue by inserting his/her will get a rise out of many a maven. Web addresses use the forward slash constantly.
:-)	**Smiley face and other emoticons**	Indicates emotions	Don't use an emoticon in writing other than in e-mail, a sticky note, or extremely informal communication :-). Emoticons are a bit outdated now, but your mom and dad might still use them because they can't figure out GIFs.

3.15 Everything in Its Place

Revision goal connected to standards:

Develop and strengthen writing by combining ideas to avoid redundancy, add clarity, and improve fluency.

Model Text

Lia Park and the Missing Jewel
– Written by Jenna Yoon

Teacher Considerations

Now that students are getting the hang of using DRAFT to combine, we use this lesson to focus on word choice while combining ideas. Jenna Yoon crafts beautiful description throughout *Lia Park and the Missing Jewel* while also celebrating Korean culture. During the discussion, you may choose to weave Yoon's use of descriptive word choice and how it helps the reader envision the scenes into the conversation. When students set off to do this work on their own, we invite them to determine parts in their writing where they, too, could add more description, often combining ideas to do so.

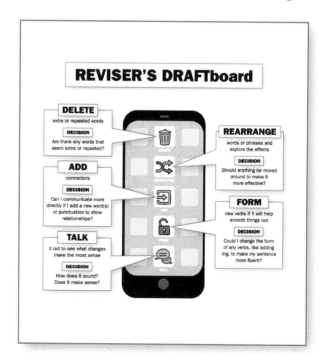

Setting the Context

In *Lia Park and the Missing Jewel*, Jenna Yoon immediately invites readers into a Taekkyeon training session with Lia Park, Joon, and their holographic instructor, Master Jinho. To set a context for students, share this information and possibly discuss the meaning of *holographic*. Read the first few paragraphs of Jenna Yoon's *Lia Park and the Missing Jewel*, which uses powerful descriptions to bring the students right into the moment. Then, share this paragraph:

> In front of me, Joon stepped in perfect rhythm with the drum. To the untrained eye, it probably looked like we were dancing. But this was actually a pretty deadly practice called Taekkyeon, a traditional Korean martial art. Even before Taekkyeon was officially listed as a UNESCO intangible cultural heritage, we've been practicing it for centuries. Keeping it alive.

Next, share with your students, "The next sentence that Jenna Yoon writes is actually a combination of ideas. Let's see how we can combine these ideas into one sentence, and compare our revision to Jenna's."

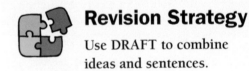 **Revision Strategy**
Use DRAFT to combine ideas and sentences.

Modeling

Using the DRAFT Reviser's Dashboard, along with the printable **3.15 Modeled Sentence Combo: Part I**, model working through combining the three sentences. Take time to discuss what the readers might be picturing in their minds as they read each sentence, including the idea of a holographic image. It may be helpful to pull up a picture from the internet of holographic images to show students what these look like. "First, let's read through each sentence and make a movie in our minds. What words or phrases help you to picture this part in your head?"

Modeling *(continued)*

A holographic image of Master Jinho was shooting out from the silver box.

Joon glanced at the image.

The silver box was in the middle of the room.

"Now we can use DRAFT to help us combine the sentences. Let's spend some time talking this out." Review the DRAFT mnemonic as needed. "I see the word *image* twice. I'm sure I could revise this so there is only one *image*. Talk it out with a neighbor. What else do you see is repeated? How could you rearrange the words to make the sentence sound right? Are there any other words that wouldn't make sense in our new combination?" As with previous lessons, model how to cross out words and write down possibilities, rearranging and adding new words, recording multiple versions as you work through the revision.

Once the students feel like they have an effective combination, reveal the author's original sentence using the display page **3.15 Modeled Sentence Combo: Part II**. "Let's listen to the original text and see how ours is alike and different." Use the reflective questions as a guide:

- Why do you think Jenna combined the sentences in this way?
- Is there another combination that would be effective?
- Why do you think your combination was different from or the same as Jenna's?
- If your combination was different from Jenna's, which do you prefer, and why?

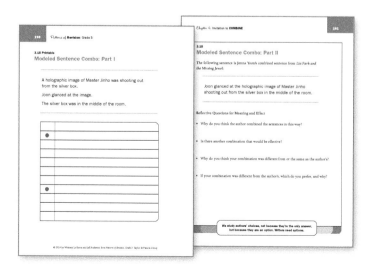

Collaborating Through Conversation

Distribute the printable **3.15 Invitation to Combine: Part I** to each student. Following the directions provided and using DRAFT, students collaborate through conversation with one or more classmates to combine the sentences into one. Remind them to picture the scene in their minds, noticing Jenna Yoon's use of imagery. Students use the workspace on the printable to record multiple versions, ultimately deciding which one is most effective. When ready, students compare their choices with others. Then, using the display page **3.15 Invitation to Combine: Part II**, share the author's original text for comparative analysis. Use the reflective questions to facilitate a conversation about meaning and effect.

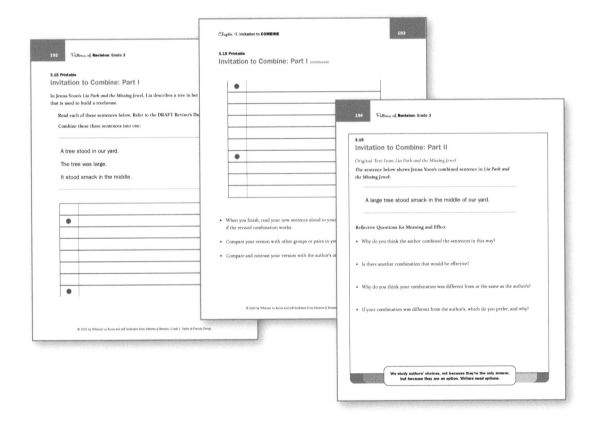

Applying Revision

Students return to a piece of writing they've been working on to play with different sentence combos, using their DRAFT Reviser's Dashboard. Students notice the different effects. If they have a hard time finding sentences in their own writing to combine, invite them to choose a place in their writing that could use some more description, like the sentences from *Lia Park and the Missing Jewel*. Once they've determined a place to add description, they can play with the possibilities of combing these descriptive ideas into a sentence.

Sharing Results

Invite students to share and celebrate their revisions in a small group. Choose one or two students to share with the class, naming what the writer did with the revision strategy: Use DRAFT to combine ideas and sentences.

3.15 Printable

Modeled Sentence Combo: Part I

A holographic image of Master Jinho was shooting out from the silver box.

Joon glanced at the image.

The silver box was in the middle of the room.

3.15

Modeled Sentence Combo: Part II

The following sentence is Jenna Yoon's combined sentence from *Lia Park and the Missing Jewel*:

Joon glanced at the holographic image of Master Jinho shooting out from the silver box in the middle of the room.

Reflective Questions for Meaning and Effect

- Why do you think the author combined the sentences in this way?

- Is there another combination that would be effective?

- Why do you think your combination was different from or the same as the author's?

- If your combination was different from the author's, which do you prefer, and why?

> We study authors' choices, not because they're the only answer, but because they are an option. Writers need options.

3.15 Printable

Invitation to Combine: Part I

In Jenna Yoon's *Lia Park and the Missing Jewel*, Lia describes a tree in her yard that is used to build a treehouse.

Read each of these sentences below. Refer to the DRAFT Reviser's Dashboard.

Combine these three sentences into one:

A tree stood in our yard.

The tree was large.

It stood smack in the middle.

●	
●	

3.15 Printable

Invitation to Combine: Part I *(continued)*

- When you finish, read your new sentence aloud to your group to see if the revised combination works.

- Compare your version with other groups or pairs in your class.

- Compare and contrast your version with the author's original text.

3.15

Invitation to Combine: Part II

Original Text from *Lia Park and the Missing Jewel*

The sentence below shows Jenna Yoon's combined sentence in *Lia Park and the Missing Jewel*:

A large tree stood smack in the middle of our yard.

Reflective Questions for Meaning and Effect

- Why do you think the author combined the sentences in this way?

- Is there another combination that would be effective?

- Why do you think your combination was different from or the same as the author's?

- If your combination was different from the author's, which do you prefer, and why?

We study authors' choices, not because they're the only answer, but because they are an option. Writers need options.

3.16 Putting Sentences Together, One by One

Revision goal connected to standards:

Develop and strengthen writing by combining ideas to avoid redundancy, add clarity, and improve fluency.

Model Text

Rise Up and Write It
- Written by Nandini Ahuja
- Illustrated by Anoosha Syed

Teacher Considerations

We love Ahuja's *Rise Up and Write It* because it focuses on advocacy, showing children how they can use their voice through writing to make a difference in their community. It also includes samples of petitions, letters, and posters representing different ways to communicate a message. In this lesson, students will continue to use DRAFT to combine ideas, ultimately forming sentences with compound subjects or compound predicates. As always, encourage a lot of talking it out, making the conversation about meaning and effect, rather than right or wrong.

Setting the Context

To set a context, share what Nandini Ahuja's *Rise Up and Write It* is about. You may choose to read the blurb on the back of the book, if you haven't already read the book aloud to your students earlier in the school year. Then read aloud the following sentence from the book where Farah leads her friends to gather signatures for a petition to make an empty neighborhood lot into a community garden.

Farah and her friends sharpened their pencils, ready for the journey ahead.

Now share with your students, "Nandini Ahuja wants to tell what happens next in a way that is not too choppy for her readers."

 Revision Strategy

Use **DRAFT** to combine ideas and sentences.

Modeling

Use the DRAFT Reviser's Dashboard, along with the printable **3.16 Modeled Sentence Combo: Part I**, to explore the three parts of the unrevised original sentence that need to be combined into one. "There are three sentences here that tell what happens next. Let's use DRAFT and see if we can make these three sentences into one. First let's read aloud the sentences."

Modeling *(continued)*

They knocked on every door.

The doors were in the neighborhood.

They shared their big idea.

"Let's spend some time talking out ways we could combine these sentences, remembering that we can use any of the DRAFT strategies to help." Refer to the DRAFT Reviser's Dashboard as needed. Model how to combine the sentences, saying things like, "I see the pronoun *they* twice. I'm sure I could revise this so there is only one *they*. Talk it out with a neighbor. What else do you see is repeated? Let's see how we might rearrange the words now. Hmm, what connector word might we add? Let's talk it out." Refer to **The Connectors** printable on page 142 as needed.

Once the students feel like they have an effective combination, display the author's original sentence using **3.16 Modeled Sentence Combo: Part II**. Invite students to compare and contrast their version with Nandini's using the reflective questions as a guide:

- Why do you think Nandini combined the sentences in this way?
- Is there another combination that would be effective?
- Why do you think your combination was different from or the same as Nandini's?
- If your combination was different from Nandini's, which do you prefer, and why?

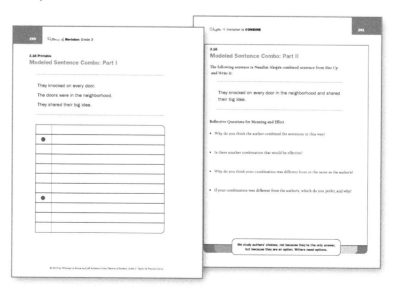

Collaborating Through Conversation

Distribute the printable **3.16 Invitation to Combine: Part I** to each student. Following the directions provided and using DRAFT, students collaborate through conversation with one or more classmates to combine the sentences into one. Remind them to use the workspace on their printable to record their different versions, talking out each one. When ready, students compare their choices with other partnerships or groups. They may choose to make changes after talking it out during this time. Then, using the display page **3.16 Invitation to Combine: Part II**, reveal the author's original sentence for comparative analysis. Use the reflective questions at the bottom of the display page to facilitate a conversation about meaning and effect.

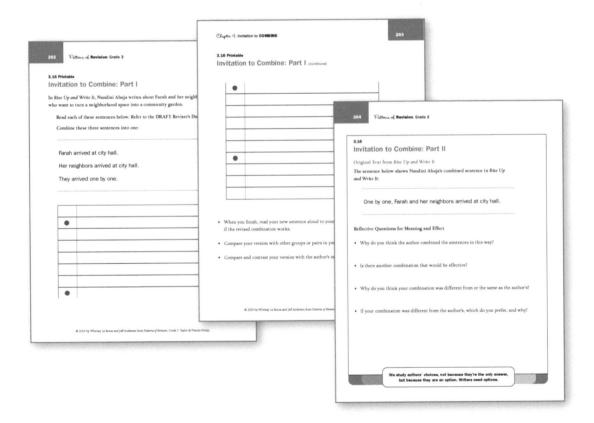

Students return to their own writing, either a draft in progress or anything from their writing notebook, to play with different sentence combos, using the DRAFT strategies. Invite writers to take a look at the actions in their sentences to see if they have multiple actions connected to just one subject. These could be combined, using a compound predicate. Or maybe they have several subjects that could be combined with just one action, using a compound subject. Remember, it isn't as important that students can name these terms as much as they notice their different effects. Invite them to refer to their **Connectors chart** for other connecting words to use when combining ideas. For those students who have a hard time finding sentences in their own writing to combine, invite them to look at their very first sentence and maybe the sentence after it. Could they be combined? If not, are there some details that could be added to one of the sentences? Talk it out to see how these new details could be combined with the sentence that is already there. Students can then repeat this process with the last sentences of their piece as well. Writers may also discover that they have a lot of repetition in a long sentence. If so, invite them to use DRAFT to break up the long sentence and then choose what should be combined afterward, as this third grader did below in Figure 3.16.

Figure 3.16

This writer noticed his introduction was repetitive and used DRAFT to break down, delete, and combine his ideas to revise into clear, effective sentences.

With partners, invite students to share and celebrate the revision they did in this lesson. Each student can then write a complimentary note to their partner, naming what they did to revise for clarity: "You made your writing more effective when you _____."

3.16 Printable

Modeled Sentence Combo: Part I

They knocked on every door.

The doors were in the neighborhood.

They shared their big idea.

●	
●	

3.16
Modeled Sentence Combo: Part II

The following sentence is Nandini Ahuja's combined sentence from *Rise Up and Write It*:

They knocked on every door in the neighborhood and shared their big idea.

Reflective Questions for Meaning and Effect

- Why do you think the author combined the sentences in this way?

- Is there another combination that would be effective?

- Why do you think your combination was different from or the same as the author's?

- If your combination was different from the author's, which do you prefer, and why?

We study authors' choices, not because they're the only answer, but because they are an option. Writers need options.

3.16 Printable

Invitation to Combine: Part I

In *Rise Up and Write It*, Nandini Ahuja writes about Farah and her neighbors, who want to turn a neighborhood space into a community garden.

Read each of these sentences below. Refer to the DRAFT Reviser's Dashboard.

Combine these three sentences into one:

Farah arrived at city hall.

Her neighbors arrived at city hall.

They arrived one by one.

3.16 Printable

Invitation to Combine: Part I *(continued)*

- When you finish, read your new sentence aloud to your group to see if the revised combination works.

- Compare your version with other groups or pairs in your class.

- Compare and contrast your version with the author's original text.

3.16
Invitation to Combine: Part II

Original Text from *Rise Up and Write It*

The sentence below shows Nandini Ahuja's combined sentence in *Rise Up and Write It*:

One by one, Farah and her neighbors arrived at city hall.

Reflective Questions for Meaning and Effect

- Why do you think the author combined the sentences in this way?

- Is there another combination that would be effective?

- Why do you think your combination was different from or the same as the author's?

- If your combination was different from the author's, which do you prefer, and why?

We study authors' choices, not because they're the only answer,
but because they are an option. Writers need options.

3.17 Combining Forces: The Butterfly Effect

Lesson Overview

Revision goal connected to standards:

Develop and strengthen writing by combining ideas to avoid redundancy, add clarity, and improve fluency.

Model Text

Butterfly for a King: Saving Hawaii's Kamehameha Butterflies
– Written by Susan L. Roth and Cindy Trumbore

Teacher Considerations

As we continue to support writers to apply DRAFT to combine ideas and sentences, we up the ante by folding in a more complex combination of ideas. Additionally, this lesson invites students to think about how authors begin their sentences in different ways, such as with an opener.

Opener, sentence .

As students talk it out to rearrange the words in the sentence, invite them to consider other ways to start the sentence, moving groups of words, or phrases, around and adding the comma to separate and connect. Be sure to spend quite some time talking it out, showing students that working through this is heavy but powerful revision.

Patterns of Power Lesson 6.1: Verbs Move: Verbs Mean Action gives students other examples of how authors list a series of actions in a more simplified way.

Setting the Context

In *Butterfly for a King: Saving Hawaii's Kamehameha Butterflies*, Susan L. Roth and Cindy Trumbore share the story of how a group of fifth graders saved the Kamehameha butterfly, native to Hawaii. To set a context, read aloud this excerpt from *Butterfly for a King*:

In 2009, six fifth-grade students in Hawaii thought there should be an official state insect. Naturally, they considered the Kamehameha butterfly. They also thought about Hawaii's happy face spider (even though spiders are not insects). Luckily for the Kamehameha butterfly, the students decided people like butterflies more than spiders.

After reading aloud the excerpt, say something like this: "Now these authors want to tell what the students did next. They could write these actions using a lot of sentences, or they could combine the ideas or actions into one sentence. Writers make choices."

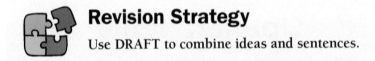 **Revision Strategy**
Use DRAFT to combine ideas and sentences.

Modeling

Use the DRAFT Reviser's Dashboard, along with the printable **3.17 Modeled Sentence Combo: Part I**, to explore the five sentences that represent the ideas in Roth and Trumbore's original sentence. "Wow! Here are five sentences that show what the students did next in this story. Let's play around with DRAFT to see how we can revise these ideas and combine them into one sentence. First, let's read aloud the sentences."

The students prepared talks.

The students wrote letters to lawmakers.

The students then went to the state capitol.

The state capitol is in Honolulu.

The students did all of this with their teacher's help.

"Let's spend some time talking out ways we could combine these sentences, using any of the DRAFT strategies to help." Refer to the DRAFT Reviser's Dashboard as needed. Model how to combine the sentences, noticing the repetition of *the students* and then the actions *the students* took (Figure 3.17). "Talk it out with a neighbor. What else do you see? How could you rearrange the words and add connectors?" As students share their ideas, model by recording their thoughts in the workspace provided on the printable to collect different ideas, forming a variety of possible sentences, and talking them out to see which ones are more fluent than others. You may choose to spend more time on rearranging parts of the sentence, talking out how the phrase *with their teacher's help* could go at the end or even at the beginning of the sentence. "Hmm, we're noticing that we could say *with their teacher's help* somewhere in this sentence, too. Where might we place that phrase? Let's talk through some possibilities."

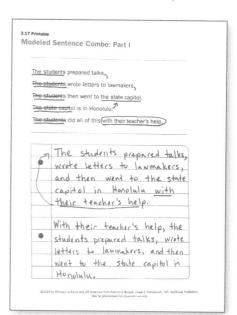

Figure 3.17

Teacher modeling the recording of several versions of the sentence while using DRAFT to help.

(continues)

Modeling *(continued)*

Honor the variety of ways students suggest combining the information, seeking clarity. Remember the importance of the instructional conversation and, as always, avoid positioning this as a task-oriented checklist, focusing instead on an authentic interaction that explores *how* we delete, rearrange, add connectors, form new verbs (maybe), and talk it out. This conversation shows that writers have choices, and it is up to them to determine how their ideas should sound when read aloud.

When the students feel like they have an effective combination, reveal the authors' original sentence using the display page **3.17 Modeled Sentence Combo: Part II**. Invite students to compare and contrast their version with Roth and Trumbore's, using the reflective questions as a guide:

- Why do you think Susan and Cindy combined the sentences in this way?
- Is there another combination that would be effective?
- Why do you think your combination was different from or the same as Susan and Cindy's?
- If your combination was different from the authors', which do you prefer, and why?

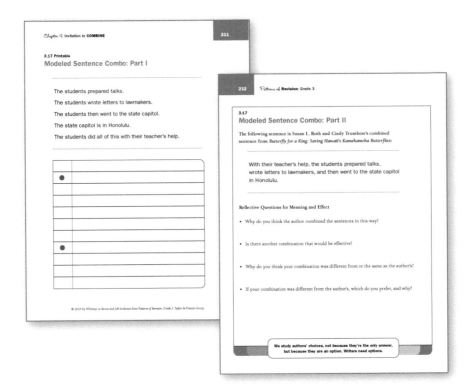

Collaborating Through Conversation

Distribute the printable **3.17 Invitation to Combine: Part I** to each student. Following the directions provided while using DRAFT, students collaborate through conversation with one or more classmates to combine the sentences into one. Remind them to really spend some time talking out the rearranging part, considering different ways to start the sentence. Have them record all of their ideas in the workspace of the printable, demonstrating the heavy revision they have worked through. When ready, students compare their choices with other partnerships or groups. Using the display page **3.17 Invitation to Combine: Part II**, show the authors' original text for comparative analysis. Use the reflective questions at the bottom to facilitate a conversation about meaning and effect.

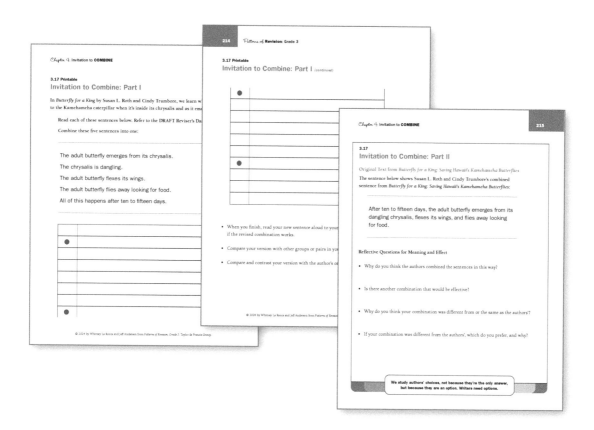

Applying Revision

As students return to their own writing, they may find some parts of their writing that are redundant, but they may not. In this case, invite them to think about what else they want their reader to know. Do they have additional ideas that can be combined with what they already have on paper? They can jot these ideas on a sticky note and then choose one to combine with a sentence or idea they have in their piece using their DRAFT Reviser's Dashboard to help. Invite them to work with a partner and consider how they are starting their sentences, rearranging parts of their sentences in different ways. Students notice the different effects and try out different versions.

Sharing Results

To celebrate the revision writers did in this lesson, invite them to share one of their newly combined sentences with a partner and record it on a sentence strip. Display the sentence strips on a wall, door, or file cabinet with a title: "We Use DRAFT to Revise!"

3.17 Printable
Modeled Sentence Combo: Part I

The students prepared talks.

The students wrote letters to lawmakers.

The students then went to the state capitol.

The state capitol is in Honolulu.

The students did all of this with their teacher's help.

3.17

Modeled Sentence Combo: Part II

The following sentence is Susan L. Roth and Cindy Trumbore's combined sentence from *Butterfly for a King: Saving Hawaii's Kamehameha Butterflies*:

With their teacher's help, the students prepared talks, wrote letters to lawmakers, and then went to the state capitol in Honolulu.

Reflective Questions for Meaning and Effect

- Why do you think the author combined the sentences in this way?

- Is there another combination that would be effective?

- Why do you think your combination was different from or the same as the author's?

- If your combination was different from the author's, which do you prefer, and why?

> **We study authors' choices, not because they're the only answer, but because they are an option. Writers need options.**

3.17 Printable

Invitation to Combine: Part I

In *Butterfly for a King* by Susan L. Roth and Cindy Trumbore, we learn what happens to the Kamehameha caterpillar when it's inside its chrysalis and as it emerges.

Read each of these sentences below. Refer to the DRAFT Reviser's Dashboard.

Combine these five sentences into one:

The adult butterfly emerges from its chrysalis.

The chrysalis is dangling.

The adult butterfly flexes its wings.

The adult butterfly flies away looking for food.

All of this happens after ten to fifteen days.

(continues)

3.17 Printable

Invitation to Combine: Part I *(continued)*

- When you finish, read your new sentence aloud to your group to see if the revised combination works.

- Compare your version with other groups or pairs in your class.

- Compare and contrast your version with the author's original text.

3.17

Invitation to Combine: Part II

Original Text from *Butterfly for a King: Saving Hawaii's Kamehameha Butterflies*

The sentence below shows Susan L. Roth and Cindy Trumbore's combined
sentence from *Butterfly for a King: Saving Hawaii's Kamehameha Butterflies*:

After ten to fifteen days, the adult butterfly emerges from its
dangling chrysalis, flexes its wings, and flies away looking
for food.

Reflective Questions for Meaning and Effect

- Why do you think the authors combined the sentences in this way?

- Is there another combination that would be effective?

- Why do you think your combination was different from or the same as the authors'?

- If your combination was different from the authors', which do you prefer, and why?

> We study authors' choices, not because they're the only answer,
> but because they are an option. Writers need options.

3.18 Combine to Make Ideas Bloom

Lesson Overview

Revision goal connected to standards:

Develop and strengthen writing by combining ideas to avoid redundancy, add clarity, and improve fluency.

Model Text

What's Inside a Flower? And Other Questions About Science and Nature
  – Written by Rachel Ignotofsky

Teacher Considerations

As students continue to use their DRAFT Reviser's Dashboard to combine ideas and sentences in this lesson, we challenge them to add the connector *to* in order *to form* an infinitive verb. An infinitive is the most basic form of a verb—the one listed in dictionaries. The verb is preceded by *to* (*to* listen, *to* read, *to* write). We invite students to visualize what the author is showing us with each sentence, and then think through what the subject does and why. Using this information to combine with DRAFT will center students on meaning and help them see another way writers combine their ideas. Finally, if you haven't encountered it together yet, this lesson will likely begin an initial conversation about the *forming new verbs* work your writers will do in future grades with the **F** from their DRAFT Reviser's Dashboard, as they consider how the verb *attract* is used and how it could be changed to *to attract* when combining.

Setting the Context

In *What's Inside a Flower? And Other Questions About Science and Nature*, Rachel Ignotofsky shares information about flowers throughout this beautifully written nonfiction text. To set a context, read aloud this excerpt from *What's Inside a Flower? And Other Questions About Science and Nature*:

Flowers attract pollinators in different ways. Many flowers have colorful petals. They are like neon signs saying "Nectar's here!"

Then explain to your students that Rachel Ignotofsky has more information to share about flowers attracting pollinators, and she has chosen to combine these details into one sentence.

 Revision Strategy

Use **DRAFT** to combine ideas and sentences.

Modeling

Using the DRAFT Reviser's Dashboard, along with the printable **3.18 Modeled Sentence Combo: Part I**, explore the three parts of the unrevised original sentence that, together, you will combine into one. "There are three sentences here. Let's play around with revision and see if we can make these three sentences into one. First let's read aloud the sentences."

(continues)

Modeling *(continued)*

Some flowers have strong smells.

Strong smells attract pollinators.

Some flowers use the strong smells.

"Let's spend some time talking out ways we could combine these sentences, remembering that we can use any of the DRAFT strategies that help." Refer to the DRAFT Reviser's Dashboard as needed. Model how to combine the sentences, saying things like, "I see the words *some flowers* twice. I'm sure we could revise this so there is only one set of *some flowers*. Are there any other words that are repeated? What about words that could be added? Talk it out with a neighbor. What would make sense here?" Guide the students through a conversation about the possibilities. "Let's try to visualize what the author is showing us with these ideas. Some flowers have strong smells that attract pollinators. That could work so far, but what does the last sentence say? How might we rearrange the sentence to add in this information?"

When ready, display **3.18 Modeled Sentence Combo: Part II** to reveal Ignotofsky's original text and guide students through a conversation of compare and contrast, using the reflective questions as a guide:

- Why do you think Rachel combined the sentences in this way?
- Is there another combination that would be effective?
- Why do you think your combination was different from or the same as Rachel's?
- If your combination was different from Rachel's, which do you prefer, and why?

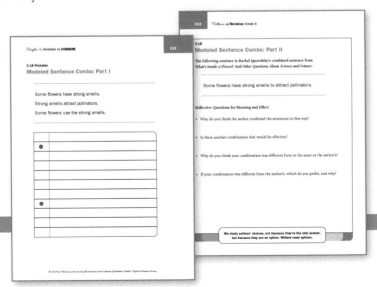

Collaborating Through Conversation

Distribute the printable **3.18 Invitation to Combine: Part I** to each student. Following the directions provided and using DRAFT, students collaborate through conversation with one or more classmates to combine the sentences into one. Remind them to visualize what the author is showing them with the sentences and how those ideas could be combined into one sentence. Students write multiple versions in the workspace of the printable as they talk it out. When ready, writers compare their choices with other partnerships or groups. Using the display page **3.18 Invitation to Combine: Part II**, share the author's original text for comparative analysis. Refer to the reflective questions while facilitating a conversation about meaning and effect.

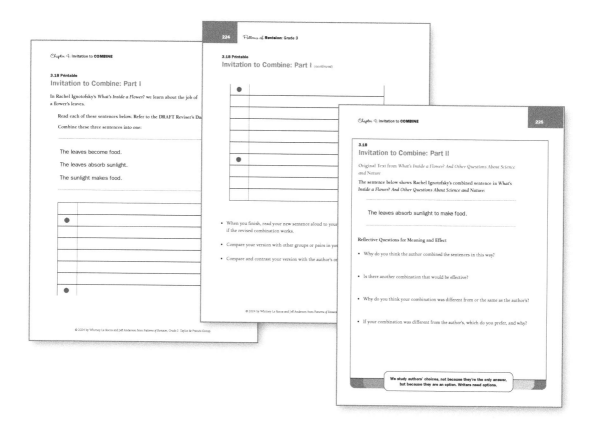

Applying Revision

Students return to their own writing, either a draft they are working on or anything in their writer's notebook, to play with different sentence combinations, using the DRAFT strategies. They may decide to use an infinitive verb when combining, or they may notice multiple actions that could be combined into a series as learned in previous lessons. When combining, writers have choices and don't have to do exactly what the mentor author has done. Students notice and play with the different effects. As with previous lessons, if students don't see any sentences in their piece that can be combined, invite them to add a new sentence to it with a combination of details or ideas.

Sharing Results

Invite students to celebrate the revision they did to their personal writing in this lesson by having them sit in a circle in groups of four. They number off and the teacher calls out a number of who will share first. After the first student shares, they choose the next person in their group to share. Continue in this way until everyone has shared with their groups.

3.18 Printable

Modeled Sentence Combo: Part I

Some flowers have strong smells.

Strong smells attract pollinators.

Some flowers use the strong smells.

3.18

Modeled Sentence Combo: Part II

The following sentence is Rachel Ignotofsky's combined sentence from
What's Inside a Flower? And Other Questions About Science and Nature:

Some flowers have strong smells to attract pollinators.

Reflective Questions for Meaning and Effect

• Why do you think the author combined the sentences in this way?

• Is there another combination that would be effective?

• Why do you think your combination was different from or the same as the author's?

• If your combination was different from the author's, which do you prefer, and why?

> **We study authors' choices, not because they're the only answer,**
> **but because they are an option. Writers need options.**

3.18 Printable

Invitation to Combine: Part I

In Rachel Ignotofsky's *What's Inside a Flower?* we learn about the job of a flower's leaves.

Read each of these sentences below. Refer to the DRAFT Reviser's Dashboard.

Combine these three sentences into one:

_____

The leaves become food.

The leaves absorb sunlight.

The sunlight makes food.

_____

(continues)

3.18 Printable

Invitation to Combine: Part I (continued)

- When you finish, read your new sentence aloud to your group to see if the revised combination works.

- Compare your version with other groups or pairs in your class.

- Compare and contrast your version with the author's original text.

3.18

Invitation to Combine: Part II

Original Text from *What's Inside a Flower? And Other Questions About Science and Nature*

The sentence below shows Rachel Ignotofsky's combined sentence in *What's Inside a Flower? And Other Questions About Science and Nature:*

The leaves absorb sunlight to make food.

Reflective Questions for Meaning and Effect

- Why do you think the author combined the sentences in this way?

- Is there another combination that would be effective?

- Why do you think your combination was different from or the same as the author's?

- If your combination was different from the author's, which do you prefer, and why?

We study authors' choices, not because they're the only answer, but because they are an option. Writers need options.

3.19 Dreaming of Better Sentences

Lesson Overview

Revision goal connected to standards:

Develop and strengthen writing by combining ideas to avoid redundancy, add clarity, and improve fluency.

Model Text

Barefoot Dreams of Petra Luna
  – Written by Alda P. Dobbs

Teacher Considerations

Now that third graders have had multiple opportunities to practice combining ideas and sentences in different ways using DRAFT, we use this lesson to showcase joining those two sentences with a comma and coordinating conjunction to form a compound sentence. When we work on compound sentences with students, we like to introduce the FANBOYS (see image below), which gives writers even more options when revising with compound sentences and helps them see how they are formed.

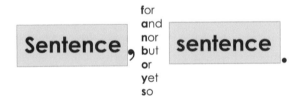

Using Alda P. Dobbs's beautifully written text *Barefoot Dreams of Petra Luna*, based on a true story set during the Mexican Revolution in 1913, students will continue their work with visualizing as they combine, discovering the two separate subjects and the two separate actions that can be merged together into one sentence.

Patterns of Power **Lessons 18.1, 18.3, and 18.4** are third-grade appropriate and invite students to dive deep into the compound sentence pattern, using the coordinating conjunctions, or FANBOYS, that are also introduced in this revision lesson.

Setting the Context

Barefoot Dreams of Petra Luna is set in 1913 when Petra Luna's town is destroyed during a revolution in Mexico, and she is separated from her parents. Told from her point of view, Petra shares her journey to safety and her dreams of learning to read. To set a context for students, share what Alda P. Dobbs's *Barefoot Dreams of Petra Luna* is about. You may choose to read the blurb on the back of the book. Then read aloud the following excerpt from Chapter 2:

> Our village had no schools, and about a year ago, a lady was sent to teach all the kids to read and write.

Then share with your students, "We are about to learn what happens next. One thing writers do is combine multiple sentences or ideas into one. Let's explore ways we can do that with this next part of Petra's story."

 Revision Strategy
Use DRAFT to combine ideas and sentences.

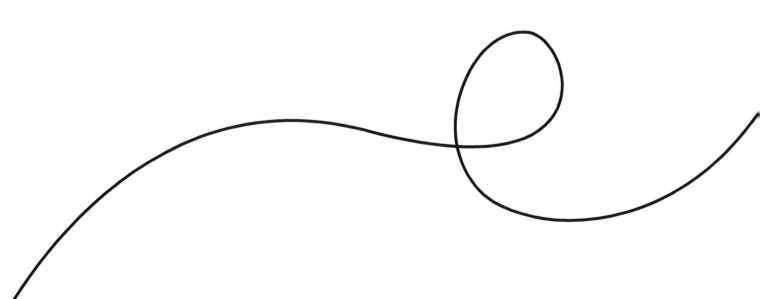

Modeling

Use the DRAFT Reviser's Dashboard, along with the printable **3.19 Modeled Sentence Combo: Part I**, to explore the five sentences that you'll combine together, ultimately becoming a compound sentence. "There are five sentences here that show Alda P. Dobbs's ideas in *Barefoot Dreams of Petra Luna*. Let's play around with revision and see if we can make these five sentences into one. First let's read aloud the sentences."

I was going to her first class.

This was the happiest day of my life.

The teacher left.

The teacher never returned.

This happened five days later.

"Hmm, let's first visualize this and spend some time talking out ways we could combine these sentences, remembering that we can use any of the DRAFT strategies to help revise the sentences to one." Guide the visualization and discussion as students consider who or what is doing the action in each sentence, discovering that there are actually two subjects (*I* and *the teacher*). "Since Petra is telling the story, we see the pronoun *I*, meaning Petra. We can see Petra is so happy about going to her very first class. But then we also can see the teacher is not there. Hmm. It looks like we have two different subjects with verbs. So let's first see how we can combine the sentences about Petra, then we can look at how we might combine the sentences about the teacher." Review the DRAFT mnemonic as needed.

Honor the suggestions writers share, writing down some possibilities on the workspace of the printable, thinking aloud as you write. Then, work through combining the two big ideas together into one sentence. "Well, look at this. Now we have two big ideas: *I was going to her first class on the happiest day of my life* and *Five days later, the teacher left* and *never returned*. OK. Let's use DRAFT to keep going

Figure 3.19

3.19 Printable
Modeled Sentence Combo: Part I

I was going to her first class. ¿on
This was the happiest day of my life.
The teacher left. ¿and
The teacher never returned.
This happened five days later.

FANBOYS
but

- I was going to her first class on the happiest day of my life, but the teacher left five days later and never returned.

- On the happiest day of my life, I was going to her first class, but five days later, the teacher left and never returned.

©2024 by Whitney La Rocca and Jeff Anderson from *Patterns of Revision, Grade 3*. Portsmouth, NH: Stenhouse Publishers. May be photocopied for classroom use only.

Modeling *(continued)*

here and combine these ideas into one sentence. What connector word could we add? What about punctuation? Is there anything else we can rearrange? Let's talk it out." Providing a list of connector words as well as the compound sentence visual will help students talk through this revision. (See **The Connectors** printable on page 142 and the compound sentence visual on page 226.)

Keep in mind, this discussion and revision practice are not about doing it exactly like Dobbs ended up writing it. It's about meaning and effect, rather than right or wrong. Continue to talk it out with students, rearranging phrases, to come up with an effective way to combine the ideas. Writers have choices. The important work the students do here is considering their options and talking through the possibilities. It is OK if they don't think to insert *five days later* after the conjunction. They may decide to put *five days later* at the end of the sentence. Both options work. As a class, you may end up writing something like Figure 3.19.

When ready, reveal the author's original sentence using the display page **3.19 Modeled Sentence Combo: Part II**, and compare and contrast the class version with Alda's, using the reflective questions as a guide:

- Why do you think the author combined the sentences in this way?
- Is there another combination that would be effective?
- Why do you think your combination was different from or the same as the author's?
- If your combination was different from the author's, which do you prefer, and why?

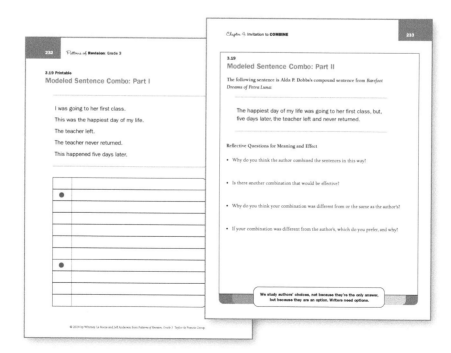

Collaborating Through Conversation

Distribute the printable **3.19 Invitation to Combine: Part I** to each student. Following the directions provided along with DRAFT, students collaborate through conversation with one or more classmates to combine the sentences into one. Invite them to take a moment to really visualize what is happening in the sentences, taking into consideration who or what the subject is and if there is more than one. As they use DRAFT, remind them of the compound sentence visual, too. Students use the workspace on their printable to jot down their possibilities. When ready, students compare their choices with other partnerships or groups. Then, using the display page **3.19 Invitation to Combine: Part II**, reveal the author's original text for comparative analysis. Use the reflective questions to facilitate a conversation about meaning and effect.

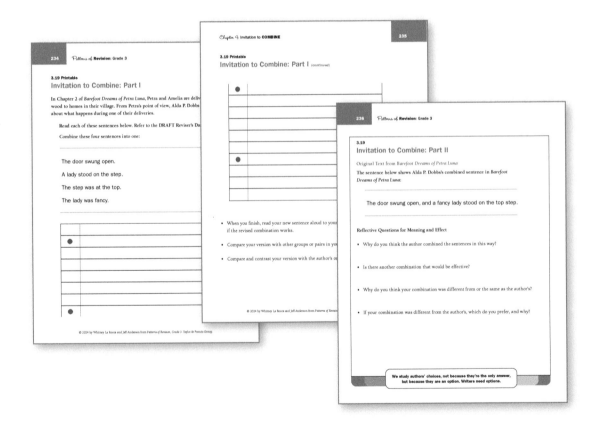

Applying Revision

Students return to their own writing, either a draft they are working on, a reading response, a poem, or anything in their writer's notebook, to play with different sentence combinations, using the DRAFT strategies. Since this lesson focuses on combining to form compound sentences, invite students to look for sentences that are related in some way, even if they have different subjects. They can refer to the compound sentence visual with the FANBOYS to consider the connectors they might use to combine their sentences. Students notice the different effects. They may choose to form compound sentences, but they may not. That is OK! If students have a hard time finding sentences in their own writing to combine, invite them to choose one part of their piece to focus on. Is there a sentence that can be added to the paragraph? What detail could be added to help the reader visualize more clearly? Can that addition be combined with a sentence already in the piece? Invite students to talk it out with a partner as needed.

Sharing Results

Roll out the red carpet for this lesson celebration! Lay a long piece of red butcher paper on the floor of your classroom, creating a red carpet that leads to the author's chair or stool. Each student walks the red carpet to the author's chair and shares their revision with the class. The audience claps for each writer, celebrating the revisions made through combining ideas and sentences.

3.19 Printable

Modeled Sentence Combo: Part I

I was going to her first class.

This was the happiest day of my life.

The teacher left.

The teacher never returned.

This happened five days later.

●	
●	

3.19
Modeled Sentence Combo: Part II

The following sentence is Alda P. Dobbs's compound sentence from *Barefoot Dreams of Petra Luna*:

The happiest day of my life was going to her first class, but, five days later, the teacher left and never returned.

Reflective Questions for Meaning and Effect

- Why do you think the author combined the sentences in this way?

- Is there another combination that would be effective?

- Why do you think your combination was different from or the same as the author's?

- If your combination was different from the author's, which do you prefer, and why?

We study authors' choices, not because they're the only answer, but because they are an option. Writers need options.

3.19 Printable

Invitation to Combine: Part I

In Chapter 2 of *Barefoot Dreams of Petra Luna*, Petra and Amelia are delivering wood to homes in their village. From Petra's point of view, Alda P. Dobbs writes about what happens during one of their deliveries.

Read each of these sentences below. Refer to the DRAFT Reviser's Dashboard.

Combine these four sentences into one:

The door swung open.

A lady stood on the step.

The step was at the top.

The lady was fancy.

3.19 Printable

Invitation to Combine: Part I *(continued)*

- When you finish, read your new sentence aloud to your group to see if the revised combination works.

- Compare your version with other groups or pairs in your class.

- Compare and contrast your version with the author's original text.

3.19

Invitation to Combine: Part II

Original Text from *Barefoot Dreams of Petra Luna*

The sentence below shows Alda P. Dobbs's combined sentence in *Barefoot Dreams of Petra Luna*:

The door swung open, and a fancy lady stood on the top step.

Reflective Questions for Meaning and Effect

- Why do you think the author combined the sentences in this way?

- Is there another combination that would be effective?

- Why do you think your combination was different from or the same as the author's?

- If your combination was different from the author's, which do you prefer, and why?

We study authors' choices, not because they're the only answer, but because they are an option. Writers need options.

3.20 Sentence Combining Is a Slam Dunk

Lesson Overview

Revision goal connected to standards:

Develop and strengthen writing by combining ideas to avoid redundancy, add clarity, and improve fluency.

Model Text

Above the Rim: How Elgin Baylor Changed Basketball
- Written by Jen Bryant
- Illustrated by Frank Morrison

Teacher Considerations

We use this final lesson to invite students to create complex sentences with their combinations. It will be important to continue the use of **The Connectors chart** alongside the DRAFT Reviser's Dashboard as students work through the choices they have as writers. You may choose to focus their attention on the connectors that are listed on the chart down the right-hand side under Subordinating Conjunctions and the Function/Examples.

Although we don't spend a lot of time teaching third graders how to write a complex sentence, they often will write them without knowing what they are. The most important thing here is for them to consider which connectors would work best to combine the ideas. They will go deeper with analyzing and composing complex sentences as they get older.

Patterns of Power **Lessons 20.1, 20.2, 20.3, 20.4, and 20.5** give third graders more opportunities to explore complex sentence patterns as well as the use and placement of subordinating conjunctions, or AAAWWUBBIS words.

Setting the Context

In *Above the Rim: How Elgin Baylor Changed Basketball*, Jen Bryant shares the story of Elgin Baylor, one of the first professional Black players of the NBA, who advocated for civil rights and the equal treatment of all NBA players. To set a context, read aloud this excerpt from Jen Bryant's *Above the Rim: How Elgin Baylor Changed Basketball*:

> On a steamy summer day in 1945, a boy and his brothers played stickball in the street. There were plenty of nice parks in Washington, D.C., where people swam or played tennis, basketball, and baseball. But the child was black, and those parks were "whites only."

Then share with your students, "Jen Bryant wants to tell what happens next that changed Elgin's life. One way she can do this is to combine some ideas into one sentence."

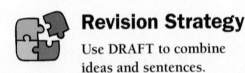 **Revision Strategy**

Use DRAFT to combine ideas and sentences.

Modeling

Use the DRAFT chart, along with the printable **3.20 Modeled Sentence Combo: Part I**, to explore the three parts of the unrevised original sentence that need to be combined into one. "There are three sentences here that show Jen Bryant's ideas in her book about Elgin Baylor. Let's play around with revision, using DRAFT, and see if we can combine these three sentences into one. First let's read them aloud and visualize what they are showing us."

> He was fourteen.
>
> A hoop appeared in the field.
>
> The field was down the street.

Modeling *(continued)*

"Let's spend some time talking out ways we could combine these sentences, remembering that we can use any of the DRAFT strategies to help." Review the DRAFT mnemonic as needed, and guide students to the right-hand side of **The Connectors** printable (found on page 142) to explore their options for adding as they merge the ideas presented. Model how to combine the sentences, saying things like, "I see the phrase *the field* twice. I'm sure I could revise this so there is only one phrase that says *the field.* Talk it out with a neighbor. What else do you see? How could we rearrange the words and add connectors? Let's look at **The Connectors chart** to see some of our options." Students may suggest beginning the sentence with the subordinating conjunction *when.* This certainly works, so talk through what that could look like:

> *When he was fourteen, a hoop appeared in the field down the street.*
>
> or
>
> *When a hoop appeared in the field down the street, he was fourteen.*

Then ask which feels most effective and if there are other ways to rearrange these ideas. This conversation will show that writers have choices, and it is up to them to determine how their ideas should sound when read aloud.

Once the students feel like they have an effective combination, reveal the author's original sentence using the display page **3.20 Modeled Sentence Combo: Part II**. Invite writers to compare and contrast their version with Jen Bryant's, using the reflective questions as a guide:

- Why do you think Jen combined the sentences in this way?
- Is there another combination that would be effective?
- Why do you think your combination was different from or the same as Jen's?
- If your combination was different from Jen's, which do you prefer, and why?

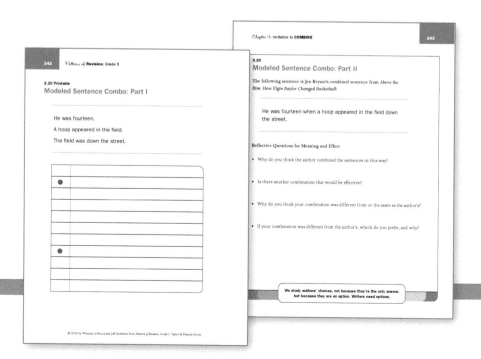

Collaborating Through Conversation

Distribute the printable **3.20 Invitation to Combine: Part I** to each student. Following the directions provided and using DRAFT, students collaborate through conversation with one or more classmates to combine the sentences into one. Remind them to visualize first to consider the grouping and rearranging of words and to use **The Connectors** printable to try out different conjunctions. When ready, writers compare their choices with other partnerships or groups. Then, using the display page **3.20 Invitation to Combine: Part II**, share the author's original text for comparative analysis. Use the reflective questions to facilitate a conversation about meaning and effect.

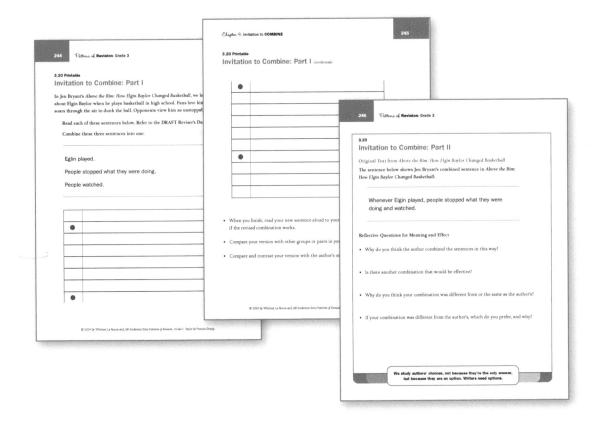

Applying Revision

Students return to their own writing to play with different sentence combinations, using the DRAFT strategies. Since this lesson focuses on combining into a complex sentence, invite students to try using different subordinating conjunctions, or AAAWWUBBIS words, as their connectors. Students notice the different effects. If they have a hard time finding sentences in their own writing to combine, invite them to create a practice box for combining their thinking. A box can be drawn directly onto the page, or writers can practice on a sticky note. Students think about two or three additional things they want their reader to know and either combine those thoughts into a new sentence or incorporate them with a sentence they already have written. For example, they may choose to write a sentence about the setting or the character if they are writing narrative. Or, if they are writing an informational piece, they might write an additional sentence of combined ideas about the topic. Perhaps they'll choose to work this new revision somewhere into their writing, or they may not. Either way, they have had the opportunity to practice combining and making choices (Figure 3.20).

Figure 3.20
This writer used DRAFT to combine several of her ideas into one sentence.

Sharing Results

Make this final lesson celebration a slam dunk! Create a space for students to share their revisions with the class or in small groups and then shoot some hoops. Using a clean, empty wastebasket in your classroom as the hoop and a wadded-up piece of paper or Wiffle Ball as the basketball, invite each student to go for the goal, tossing the ball into the basket after sharing. The audience claps for each writer, celebrating the revisions made through combining ideas and sentences.

3.20 Printable

Modeled Sentence Combo: Part I

He was fourteen.

A hoop appeared in the field.

The field was down the street.

3.20
Modeled Sentence Combo: Part II

The following sentence is Jen Bryant's combined sentence from *Above the Rim: How Elgin Baylor Changed Basketball*:

He was fourteen when a hoop appeared in the field down the street.

Reflective Questions for Meaning and Effect

- Why do you think the author combined the sentences in this way?

- Is there another combination that would be effective?

- Why do you think your combination was different from or the same as the author's?

- If your combination was different from the author's, which do you prefer, and why?

We study authors' choices, not because they're the only answer, but because they are an option. Writers need options.

3.20 Printable

Invitation to Combine: Part I

In Jen Bryant's *Above the Rim: How Elgin Baylor Changed Basketball*, we learn more about Elgin Baylor when he plays basketball in high school. Fans love him as he soars through the air to dunk the ball. Opponents view him as unstoppable.

Read each of these sentences below. Refer to the DRAFT Reviser's Dashboard.

Combine these three sentences into one:

Eglin played.

People stopped what they were doing.

People watched.

3.20 Printable

Invitation to Combine: Part I *(continued)*

- When you finish, read your new sentence aloud to your group to see if the revised combination works.

- Compare your version with other groups or pairs in your class.

- Compare and contrast your version with the author's original text.

3.20

Invitation to Combine: Part II

Original Text from *Above the Rim: How Elgin Baylor Changed Basketball*

The sentence below shows Jen Bryant's combined sentence in *Above the Rim: How Elgin Baylor Changed Basketball*:

> Whenever Elgin played, people stopped what they were doing and watched.

Reflective Questions for Meaning and Effect

- Why do you think the author combined the sentences in this way?

- Is there another combination that would be effective?

- Why do you think your combination was different from or the same as the author's?

- If your combination was different from the author's, which do you prefer, and why?

We study authors' choices, not because they're the only answer, but because they are an option. Writers need options.

Conclusion

Living in a **REVISION** Mindset

Life is a balance between holding on and letting go.

– Rumi

Revision means change. And if we're to be honest, we don't all love change—at first—and neither do third graders. Change is new. Change can be difficult. Change takes time. Third-grade writers would much prefer to write a draft and be done with it—no revision, no editing. But keep in mind, everything doesn't need to change all at once. Start in small chunks and your students will be able to handle larger and larger chunks over time.

Making the right changes in our writing is about making thoughtful decisions about what we'll keep and what we'll need to let go of. We know from professional writers that we learn the most about writing through revision. Like writing, we get better at revision by doing it. In *Patterns of Revision*, we designed the lessons to make the work of revision intriguing enough to be engaging, but also simple enough for third graders to succeed at and use. As you navigate through the lessons included here, you'll begin to see that a limited set of options within the DRAFT mnemonic gives young writers a bite-sized way into revision. An action at a time.

Patterns of Revision offers a structure with a healthy dose of conversation and open-endedness, providing the engagement that comes with choice while keeping things simple enough that students don't become overwhelmed. Challenged not frozen. Playful not avoidant. Exploring not ignoring. Over the span of the lessons, young writers are intrigued that a few moves can make great improvement.

Revision is change.

Be open.

Listen.

Allow space.

Try not to resist the changes that come your way. Instead let life live through you. And do not worry your life is turning upside down. How do you know that the side you are used to is better than the one to come?

– Rumi

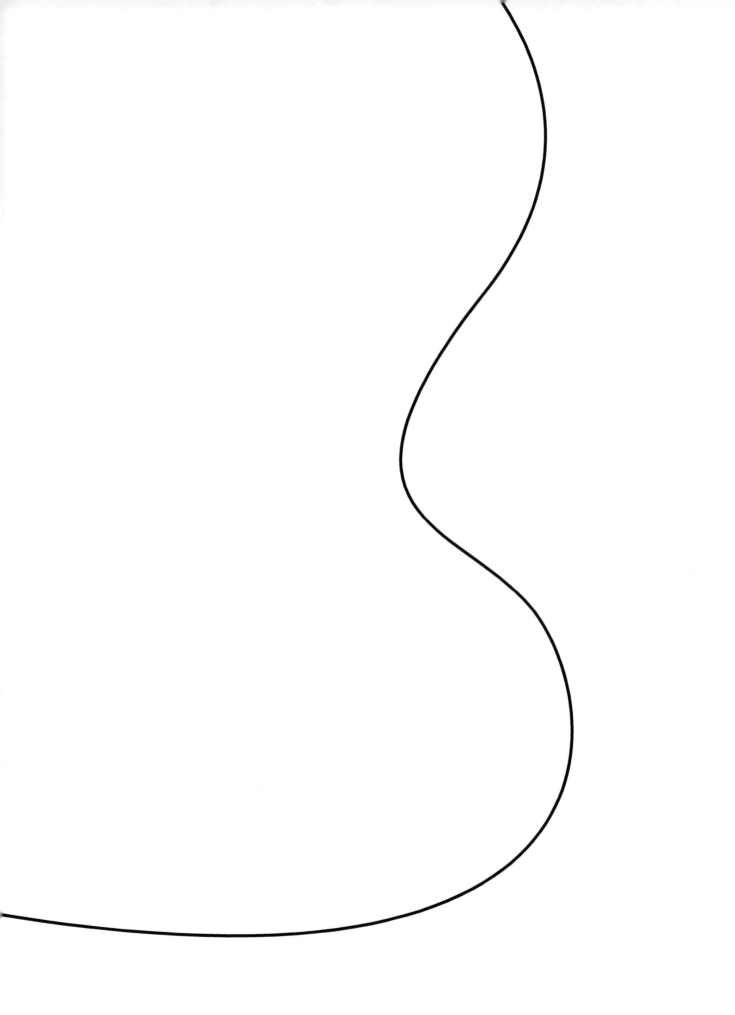

Children's Literature Bibliography

Ahuja, Nandini. 2021. *Rise Up and Write It*. New York: HarperCollins.

Anderson, Jeff. 2018. *Zack Delacruz: Upstaged*. New York: Sterling.

Bryant, Jen. 2020. *Above the Rim: How Elgin Baylor Changed Basketball*. New York: Abrams Books for Young Readers.

Burgess, Matthew. 2020. *Drawing on Walls: A Story of Keith Haring*. New York: Enchanted Lion Books.

Cooper, Brittney. 2022. *Stand Up! 10 Mighty Women Who Made a Change*. New York: Orchard Books.

Cousteau, Philippe, and Deborah Hopkinson. 2016. *Follow the Moon Home: A Tale of One Idea, Twenty Kids, and a Hundred Sea Turtles*. San Francisco: Chronicle Books.

Dillard, J. 2021. *J.D. and the Great Barber Battle*. New York: Kokila.

Dobbs, Alda P. 2022. *Barefoot Dreams of Petra Luna*. Naperville, IL: Sourcebooks Young Readers.

Faruqi, Saadia. 2021. *Yasmin the Librarian*. North Mankato, MN: Picture Window Books.

Fleming, Candace. 2022. *Crash from Outer Space*. New York: Scholastic.

Henkes, Kevin. 2021. *Billy Miller Makes a Wish*. New York: Greenwillow Books.

Ignotofsky, Rachel. 2021. *What's Inside a Flower? And Other Questions About Science and Nature*. New York: Crown Books for Young Readers.

Latham, Irene, and Karim Shamsi-Basha. 2020. *The Cat Man of Aleppo*. New York: G. P. Putnam's Sons.

Lyons, Kelly Starling. 2020. *Dream Builder: The Story of Architect Philip Freelon*. New York: Lee & Low Books.

McDaniels, Darryl "DMC." 2022. *Darryl's Dream*. New York: Random House.

Messner, Kate. 2019. *Ranger in Time: Disaster on the Titanic*. New York: Scholastic.

Nordstrom, Kristen. 2021. *Mimic Makers: Biomimicry Inventors Inspired by Nature*. Watertown, MA: Charlesbridge.

Phi, Bao. 2017. *A Different Pond*. North Mankato, MN: Capstone Young Readers.

Reynolds, Jan. 2020. *The Lion Queens of India*. New York: Lee & Low Books.

Roth, Susan L., and Cindy Trumbore. 2021. *Butterfly for a King: Saving Hawaii's Kamehameha Butterflies*. New York: Lee & Low Books.

Stiefel, Chana. 2021. *Let Liberty Rise! How America's Schoolchildren Helped Save the Statue of Liberty*. New York: Scholastic.

Yoon, Jenna. 2022. *Lia Park and the Missing Jewel*. New York: Aladdin.

Professional Bibliography

Anderson, Jeff. 2011. *10 Things Every Writer Needs to Know*. Portland, ME: Stenhouse.

Anderson, Jeff, and Deborah Dean. 2014. *Revision Decisions: Talking Through Sentences and Beyond.* Portland, ME: Stenhouse.

Anderson, Jeff, with Whitney La Rocca. 2017. *Patterns of Power: Inviting Young Writers into the Conventions of Language, Grades 1–5*. Portland, ME: Stenhouse.

Graham, Steve, and Delores Perin. 2007. *Writing Next: Effective Strategies to Improve Writing of Adolescents in Middle and High School.* A Report to Carnegie Corporation of New York. Washington, DC: Alliance for Education.

Qarooni, Nawal. 2024. *Nourish Caregiver Collaborations: Elevating Home Experiences and Classroom Practices for Collective Care.* New York: Routledge.

Vygotsky, Lev S. 1978. *Mind in Society: The Development of Higher Psychological Process.* Ed. and trans. Michael Cole, Vera John-Steiner, Sylvia Scribner, and Ellen Souberman. Cambridge, MA: Harvard University Press.

RESEARCH-BASED AND STANDARDS-ALIGNED

Patterns of POWER
FAMILY OF PROFESSIONAL BOOKS

An inquiry-based approach to grammar instruction PreK–12

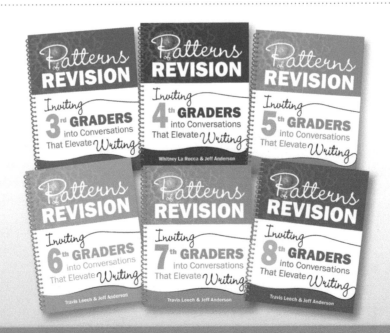

Routledge
Taylor & Francis Group
NEW YORK AND LONDON

A Stenhouse Book

CERTIFIED
CARBON
NEUTRAL®
Publication
CarbonNeutral.com

SCAN ME